M O D U L E

Cost Measurement Systems: Traditional and Contemporary Approaches

Version 1.0

AUTHORS:

Shahid Ansari
California State University Northridge

Carol Lawrence
University of Richmond

Contents
Cost Measurement Systems: Traditional and Contemporary Approaches

ISBN 0-256-26394-9

Printed in the United States of America

2 3 4 5 6 7 8 9 0   MZ   3 2 1

Cost Measurement Systems: Traditional and Contemporary Approaches

TWO PERSPECTIVES ON COSTING

"It's really not fair to compare the cost of the job we're working on now for a wastewater treatment plant in Sweden with the job we just finished for a sugar mill in Zimbabwe. The Sweden job requires heavy-duty surface finishes to withstand the exposure to severe winter weather. We've had real problems with the new weatherproof paint we're trying." The production manager of **Alfa Laval** offered this explanation at the monthly staff meeting as managers reviewed the latest cost reports. The company's plant in Richmond, Virginia, makes equipment for industrial processes that require heating and cooling of liquids during processing.

Meanwhile, across town at the **A.H. Robins** plant that produces over-the-counter and prescription cold and flu medicines sold under the brand names Robitussin and Dimetapp, managers were also reviewing cost reports. Costs in the mixing department were slowly inching upwards. The plant manager protested, "But the cost increase is only *2 cents*!" The controller responded, "With the huge quantities we produce, 2 cents per bottle adds up in a hurry. That 2 cents a bottle will increase our total cost by $360,000 this quarter, and if this keeps up, total cost for the year will be $1,440,000 more than last year!"

Everyone agreed with the plant manager when he commented, "You know, it seems we get lots of information from our accounting system, but it doesn't really tell us what we need to know. I want to know how to manage our costs proactively, not just find out after the fact they were too high!" The controller spoke up, "I know our accounting system has to change. Perhaps we can incorporate some of the more contemporary approaches to cost measurement."

A cost measurement system records, tracks, and reports information about the resources consumed by an organization in providing its customers with the goods or services they want. The primary reasons for measuring costs are to make informed strategic choices and to manage costs. A cost measurement system is part of a **strategic management accounting system**. Other functions performed by a comprehensive strategic management accounting system include the following elements:

▲ *Competitor cost estimation* that estimates the cost at which competitors are providing similar goods and services.

▲ *Value chain* costing that helps management understand what each member of the value chain[1] contributes to the total cost of providing a product or service to a customer.

▲ *Strategic cost analysis* to help management estimate the impact of pursuing different customers or markets or of investing in different production technology.

---

[1] The value chain is the linked series of activities required to provide a service or product to a customer. A comprehensive view of the value chain would begin with the extraction of raw materials and include all steps through production, delivery, use by the customer, and recycling or final disposal.

▲ STRATEGIC IMPORTANCE OF COST MEASUREMENT SYSTEMS

Information provided by a cost measurement system helps managers achieve their major strategic objectives of providing customers with high-quality products or services, at a reasonable cost, and in a timely fashion.

▲ **Quality.** Providing customers the features and reliability they want at affordable prices can be a major challenge. A cost measurement system provides data that allows managers to understand the cost of providing customers with current levels of quality. In addition, a well-designed cost measurement system should provide information to estimate the cost of adding new features desired by customers.

▲ **Cost.** The purpose of measuring costs is to manage costs. A cost measurement system helps management to understand how each of the various cross-functional processes used to produce, deliver, and support products or services contributes to costs and what factors cause costs to change. This information helps managers to focus their cost management efforts on areas that produce the greatest benefit.

▲ **Time.** Both of the firms in the opening story face key strategic issues on the time dimension of the strategic triangle. Meeting a customer's deadline for installation is critical for Alfa Laval's heat-exchanger business. Late delivery of the heat exchangers can delay the completion of other aspects of construction, causing considerable ill will and expense for the customer.

For Robins, timely introduction of new drugs is vital to ensure an adequate return on their research spending. Because of seasonal fluctuations in demand, Robins must plan carefully to have adequate supplies of cold and flu medicines available for the winter flu season. The cost systems of both companies must help them understand how delays affect their costs and profits.

When you are finished with this module, you will

▲ Appreciate the strategic importance of cost measurement systems.

▲ Recognize that organizations use different cost measurement systems because they produce different types of outputs using different production methods.

▲ Learn about key design issues such as the selection of cost objects, accounts used to track cost flows, and allocation procedures used to trace costs to cost objects.

▲ Understand how a cost measurement system converts data on resources purchased into information on resources consumed by the cost objects (customers, activities, operations, products, processes) of interest to management.

▲ Understand how traditional department-focused cost measurement systems such as job order costing and process costing differ from contemporary cost measurement systems that focus on all activities and operations required to design, produce, and deliver a product or service to a customer.

▲ Understand the technical, behavioral, and cultural attributes of traditional and contemporary cost measurement systems.

▲ NATURE OF A COST MEASUREMENT SYSTEM

The process of cost measurement is like a building process. The basic raw material is data on purchases of resources such as materials, equipment, or labor. A cost measurement system uses these data as basic building blocks, arranging them into a structure that provides managers with cost information for making strategic decisions and managing costs. Exhibit 1 depicts this view of a cost measurement system.

Exhibit 1
Cost Measurement System as a Building Process

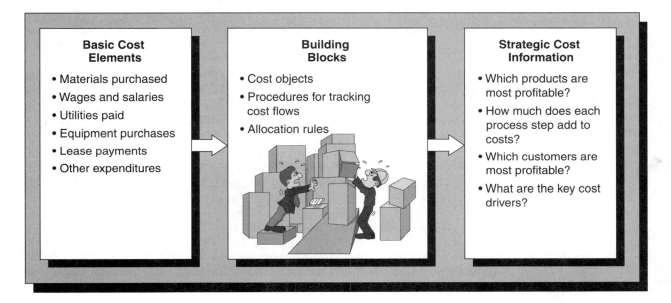

Basic Cost Elements	**Building Blocks**	**Strategic Cost Information**
• Materials purchased • Wages and salaries • Utilities paid • Equipment purchases • Lease payments • Other expenditures	• Cost objects • Procedures for tracking cost flows • Allocation rules	• Which products are most profitable? • How much does each process step add to costs? • Which customers are most profitable? • What are the key cost drivers?

The reason we need to go through this building process is that most accounting systems initially capture data on resources *purchased*, whereas managers need to know how resources are *used* to meet strategic objectives. For example, the accounting system records events such as the purchase of $100,000 worth of materials; payment of $300,000 in salary and wages (recorded in the payroll account); and purchase of $50,000 worth of new equipment. However, managers want to know how much of the $100,000 in materials; $300,000 in salaries; and $50,000 in equipment was used to produce products, how much to deliver them, and how much to support them. More important is the question: Were the revenues generated greater than the resources used in generating these revenues? This type of information is critical in determining whether a firm is producing outputs that meet or exceed customer expectations and generate profits.

The cost measurement system provides this type of managerially relevant information by creating a structure whose primary building blocks are

▲ *A set of cost objects*, processes, products, activities, customers, and so on that serve as the focus of cost accumulation and analysis.

▲ *Procedures for tracking the flow of costs* through various accounts.

▲ *Methods of allocating resources* shared by more than one cost object.

Cost Object Selection.

Most organizations use many different types of cost objects. Products, services, departments, activities, product lines and customer groups are some examples of commonly used cost objects. In a well-designed cost measurement system, cost objects correspond to management's strategic decision needs. For example, to decide which market segment to focus on, Alfa Laval's management must know which of its customers are most profitable. This factor explains why individual customer jobs are an important cost object for Alfa Laval.

Cost objects must be selected with care. Inappropriate selection of cost objects can seriously impair the usefulness of a cost measurement system. For example, until recently most organizations did not use activities as cost objects and, therefore, did not have cost data that could be used for managing critical business processes. Even today many companies use cost objects that are relevant for external financial reporting and irrelevant or misleading for internal management decision making. Measuring inventory at "full product cost" is one example of this tendency.[2]

Selecting the right cost object is particularly difficult in service industries because their output is hard to define. For example, the output of a hospital can be measured in a variety of ways. The cost measurement system might report cost per patient, per patient day, or per bed. In the early 1980s the Medicare system implemented a new reimbursement plan, based on diagnosis-related groups (DRG). The DRG system classifies each patient into one of 470 DRGs based on the nature and severity of the patient's ailment. Medicare reimburses hospitals a standard amount for each patient treated in each DRG, regardless of the actual costs the hospital incurs to treat a patient. Today many hospitals use DRGs as a major cost object for accumulating and reporting costs.[3]

Think Along

What is the cost object your university or college uses to measure the cost of educating students?[4]

Procedures for Tracking Cost Flows.

A cost measurement system provides the means of tracking costs through various accounts and intermediate cost objects to the final cost objects of interest to management. Traditional cost systems use functional areas or departments to flow and track costs to cost objects. Contemporary cost systems use activities and operations to accumulate the cost and then charge these costs to final cost objects.

Cost Allocation.

The allocation of costs that are common or shared is a critical part of the design of any cost system. Allocation rules can be quite complex. In a well-designed system the allocation scheme will reflect how costs are caused by or incurred to benefit the selected cost objects.

---

[2] The *Theory of Constraints and Throughput Accounting* module in this series develops in greater detail the difference between inventory measures for external financial reporting versus managing operations.

[3] For additional detail on hospital cost measurement systems, see Carol M. Lawrence, "The Effect of Ownership Structure and Accounting System Type on Hospital Costs," *Research in Governmental and Nonprofit Accounting*, Vol. 6, 1990, pp. 35–60.

[4] Colleges use full-time equivalent student hours. See discussion on page CMS–15.

An Example.

Let us consider a simple example to illustrate the three steps in measuring costs. Assume a hospital uses a traditional department-based cost system and wants to know the cost of treating patients who are classified in disease group 215 (i.e., the cost object is DRG 215). The first step, if the hospital uses a traditional system, is to track costs to departments. Assume we have three departments: clinic, laboratory, and administration. Further assume that for this period the total materials, supplies, salaries, and other costs traced to the three departments and their other selected statistics are as follows:

Department	Costs	Other Statistics
Clinic	$1,000,000	16,000 physician hours
Laboratory	300,000	10,000 tests
Administration	700,000	
Total	$2,000,000	

The next step is to reallocate the administration cost to the clinic and the laboratory. Let us assume that, based on a predetermined formula, these costs are split $600,000 to the clinic and $100,000 to the laboratory. The new totals are clinic $1,600,000 and laboratory $400,000. Assume that physicians spent 100 hours treating 50 patients in DRG 215 and that these patients received 150 tests. Then the cost per patient in DRG 215 can be calculated as follows:

Exam cost: [($1,600,000 ÷ 16,000 physician hours) × 100 hours] = $10,000
Lab cost: [($400,000 ÷ 10,000 tests) × 150 tests] = $ 6,000
Total cost for DRG 215 = $16,000
Cost per patient in DRG 215 (divided by 50 patients) = $ 320

Think Along

How would the hospital determine the cost of this DRG if it used activities rather than departments to collect cost?

An activity-based system would trace the $2,000,000 costs to specific activities that support treating a patient in DRG 215. The hospital in our example would have to compute the cost of admitting patients, keeping records, conducting a physical exam, performing each type of test (blood, EKG, etc.), filling prescriptions, and so on. The cost would be assigned to DRG 215 based on activities consumed by patients in this DRG. Later in the module we describe this process in greater detail.

▲ INFLUENCES ON COST MEASUREMENT SYSTEMS

Before we look at the different methods organizations use in practice to track and flow costs to final cost objects, we need to consider the reasons behind these differences. This diversity of cost systems reflects the differences in the *type of output* organizations produce and the *production methods* they use.

Type of Outputs.

Cost systems differ because each type of output requires different cost elements and a different cost management strategy. For example, in the construction industry a single major building can be a cost object and costs can be traced to it. In rice farming it does not make sense to trace costs to each grain. In automobiles the cost of purchased parts and assembling them is critical. In oil exploration the product does not require any assembled parts.

In general, organizations provide one of five types of outputs:

Extracted products are removed or drawn out of the earth by special effort or force. Oil refining, natural gas production, and coal mining are examples of extractive industries.

Processed goods are obtained by converting raw materials through substantial additional processing. Agricultural products, such as milk, cheese, butter, and ice cream, are good examples. Other examples include chemicals, paint, and cement. Robins's output (bottles of Robitussin cough syrup) fits into this category.

Assembled products are those in which numerous parts and subcomponents are put together to form a final product. Examples include cars, televisions, radios, computers, airplanes, and ships.

Fabricated products are a hybrid between processed and assembled goods. A major raw material is typically processed and then a few parts are assembled to create the final product. Examples of this group include semiconductors; machine tools and dyes; plastic toys; and paper products such as cups, stationery, and packaging. The heat exchangers produced by Alfa Laval are fabricated products.

Personal services involve the performance of duties or work for another person. Services require skilled processing or work performed by professional or service specialists. The work product of accountants, lawyers, doctors, photographers, gardeners, insurance adjusters, and waiters falls in the personal services category.

Production Methods.

Cost systems also reflect the type of production environment in which they are used. Three types of production methods have dominated the 20th century.

Craft production, universally observed prior to the Industrial Revolution, is still used for one-of-kind products produced in very small quantities. Examples are artistic works such as paintings, sculpture, and animated movies. In craft production, analysis of past costs is of limited usefulness as a guide to predicting future costs because each unit produced may be unique.

Mass production techniques have been the dominant method of manufacturing products during the 20th century. Mass production firms produce large volumes of products with little product variety. They typically use inflexible equipment and specialized labor, have long manufacturing cycles, and rely on inventories to buffer their systems from uncertainty.

Lean and **"agile"** production, developed by Japanese firms such as Toyota, is fast becoming a popular method of production in the last part of this century.[5] A lean or agile manufacturing system emphasizes flexibility and quick response. Such a system produces

---

[5] For a detailed discussion of differences between craft, mass, and lean production, see James P. Womack, Daniel T. Jones, and Daniel Roos, *The Machine That Changed the World*. Accounting implications of lean production methods are described in detail in the module *Management Accounting in the Age of Lean Production* in this series.

small volumes of products quickly and can provide a great deal of product variety. These systems typically rely on computer-aided manufacturing and use just-in-time manufacturing.

Some service industries, such as banks or insurance companies, handle large volumes of similar transactions and have characteristics of mass production. Other service industries, such as consulting, auditing, or legal services, more closely resemble a custom-order situation.

Think Along

> How do the type of output produced and the production methods used influence the design of a cost system?

Influence on Cost Measurement Systems.

While the nature of output often dictates the choice of production methods, it is not a universally fixed relationship. For example, many products today, such as automobiles, machine parts, and electronic goods, are produced using both mass and lean manufacturing methods. The choice influences the design of a cost measurement system in three major ways.

First, companies that use mass production systems have substantial inventories of raw materials, work-in-process, and finished goods. Cost measurement systems in such environments focus heavily on *inventory measurement*. In addition, because historically financial-reporting standards have dominated management reporting, manufacturing costs are often equated with product cost; only costs that can be "matched" with revenues.[6]

Second, mass production systems use unskilled labor and emphasize functional specialization. The use of unskilled labor vests all authority and responsibility with functional area managers. Managerial accounting systems reflect this orientation by using *responsibility accounting* systems. In a responsibility accounting system, managers are held responsible for managing costs within the administrative department or organizational subunit under their control. The cost centers typically are organized functionally and are referred to as *responsibility centers*. Responsibility accounting systems track costs by the person or entity responsible for costs rather than the work that gives rise to a cost. For example, assume that the warehouse in a retail department receives goods and stocks the goods on shelves. A responsibility accounting system will track all costs incurred in the warehouse—the responsibility center. However, this system will not routinely report the cost of the activities "receiving goods" and "stocking goods."

Finally, mass production systems have low product variety (few products) and large volume. Lean production systems are the opposite. They have large variety and low volumes. Mass production systems, therefore, tend to use a simple single allocation base such as labor hours and machine hours to allocate common costs to products. Lean production systems tend to use systems that use multiple allocation bases, one for each major cost pool, to allocate common costs.

▲ TRADITIONAL COST MEASUREMENT SYSTEMS

Traditional cost measurement systems reflect the influence of mass production and are characterized by excessive focus on inventory measurement, use of responsibility centers

---

[6] This is called the "matching principle." It has long governed financial reporting, and it asserts that inventory or product costs should include only costs that can be matched with revenues generated. In practice, therefore, only production costs are part of product costs, since they are easy to match with revenues.

for cost tracking, and a single base for allocating indirect or common costs. Many organizations use some variant of two popular forms of traditional cost measurement systems: job-order costing and process costing. In practice most cost systems are hybrid and combine features of both job-order and process costing. To understand their differences, however, we will illustrate job-order and process costing in their pure forms.

Increasingly, organizations are modifying or redesigning their systems to match changes in their production systems or to meet the changing needs of their competitive environment. We will use the two firms from our opening story (Alfa Laval and A.H. Robins) to describe traditional cost measurement systems and their operation and then show how these firms might design contemporary cost measurement systems.

Job-Order Costing—Alfa Laval.

In a job cost system, the primary cost object is a customer job. Job costs provide the information necessary to compute unit product costs.

Alfa Laval is a classic example of a firm that would use job-order costing.[7] One of its products is a heat exchanger used in industrial processes that must change the temperature of liquids during processing.[8] Each customer job is unique and starts with the development of detailed product specifications based on a customer's special requirements. The *engineering* department performs this function.

The production of a heat exchanger involves three manufacturing processes. First, sheet metal is stamped into plates. These plates are then moved from the *stamping* department to the *assembly* department where the plates, frames, and cover are assembled. Next, the *testing* department runs reliability tests on the assembled units. Alfa Laval's *customer support* department installs the units at the customer's site and trains customer personnel in the operation and maintenance of the units. We will illustrate a traditional cost measurement system for Alfa Laval by discussing two orders: eight units for a waste-water-treatment plant in Sweden and six units for a sugar mill in Zimbabwe. The Zimbabwe job is complete, but the heat exchangers for the Sweden job are still in process.

As stated earlier, traditional job-order costing defines *product costs* as costs that can be carried on the balance sheet as the asset inventory. Therefore, *only manufacturing costs are considered part of the product cost* for valuing inventory and calculating the cost of goods sold. All other costs are referred to as "period costs." Also, all costs are traced to functions and departments and from there to customer jobs and units produced. Exhibit 2 graphically depicts the cost tracking that occurs in a traditional job cost system.

Think Along

> How can Alfa Laval determine the manufacturing cost of the heat exchangers for the two jobs?

As the box at the far left of Exhibit 2 shows, cost tracking starts when resources (materials, labor, machinery, buildings, etc.) are acquired by an organization. Resources purchased are originally recorded in the accounting records by cost elements (materials, wages, etc.).

---

[7] We use Alfa Laval and Robins for illustrative purposes only. All numbers are fictitious. The description here has been adapted for pedagogical purposes. We do not claim, nor are we attempting, to provide a detailed and accurate description of their cost systems. No criticism of their systems is implied by this illustration.

[8] To see a picture of a plate heat exchanger, visit Alfa Laval's website at http://www.alfalaval.com/alfalaval/therm/thhome1.htm.

Exhibit 2
Cost Flows in Traditional Job-Order Costing

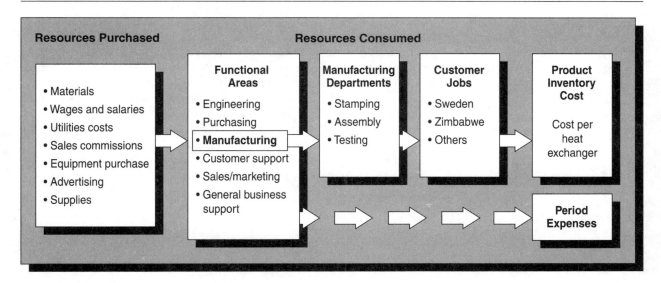

The cost system then traces these costs to the intermediate building blocks of functional areas, departments, and jobs. In traditional systems only resources consumed in manufacturing a heat exchanger are part of the job cost and unit product cost. Other cost elements, such as sales and marketing and general business support, are called period costs and are not traced to jobs or products. Instead, they are treated as expenses on the income statement.

The first step, therefore, is to identify those resources that are used by the manufacturing function. In addition, the logic of responsibility accounting requires that resources consumed within manufacturing be traced to the specific responsibility unit that uses these resources. The responsibility units are often called cost centers. Often a cost center also represents an organizational department headed by a manager who is responsible for managing costs in that cost center. As Exhibit 3 shows, Alfa Laval's manufacturing function has three cost centers: stamping, assembly, and testing. All resources consumed by these cost centers are broken into those that can be uniquely traced to particular customer jobs (direct materials and direct labor) and those that are common (manufacturing overhead costs) and must be allocated to jobs.

Exhibit 3
Analysis of Manufacturing Costs by Departments and Cost Categories.

	Stamping	Assembly	Testing	Totals
Direct materials issued	$3,200,000	$1,200,000	$300,000	$4,700,000
Direct labor	250,000	750,000	150,000	1,150,000
Manufacturing overhead	1,625,000	4,875,000	975,000	7,475,000
Total costs	**$5,075,000**	**$6,825,000**	**$1,425,000**	**$13,325,000**

From production departments Alfa Laval's system traces costs to individual customer jobs. This step requires the use of job numbers. Assume that the Sweden job is assigned the number WE-046-12-061-97 (WE signifies western Europe, 046 is the country code for Sweden, 12 is the sales territory within Sweden, 061 is the customer number, and 97 is the year the job started). The Zimbabwe job number is SA-263-15-026-97.

Job numbers serve both as authorization codes and as the means of tracing costs to jobs. When materials are requisitioned, the requisition slips indicate the department and the job that requested the materials. Engineers record the time they spend on each job on their time sheets. Machine operators and workers pass machine-readable bar codes on their identification badges through a bar code reader each time they change from one job to another.

Manufacturing overhead costs are indirect with respect to individual jobs. These costs are allocated to the two jobs using any one of several common allocation methods. For the example in Exhibit 4, we have assumed that manufacturing overhead is charged to jobs using machine hours in the stamping and testing departments and direct labor hours in the assembly department. A predetermined rate is used to charge overhead to jobs, and the difference between actual overhead incurred in a period and the amount charged to jobs is charged to the cost of good sold account. A full explanation of the allocation of common and shared costs is beyond the scope of this module. It is the subject of two separate modules in this series.[9] Exhibit 4 shows the results of this process.

Exhibit 4
Analysis of Manufacturing Costs by Jobs

	Sweden Job WE-046-12-061-97	Zimbabwe Job SA-263-15-026-97	Other Jobs	Totals
Direct materials				
Stamping	$384,000	$192,000	$2,624,000	$3,200,000
Assembly	108,000	72,000	1,020,000	1,200,000
Testing	54,000	18,000	228,000	300,000
Direct labor				
Stamping	5,000	3,000	242,000	250,000
Assembly	5,000	26,250	718,750	750,000
Testing	24,000	16,500	109,500	150,000
Manufacturing overhead*				
Stamping	48,750	32,500	1,543,750	1,625,000
Assembly	292,500	146,250	4,436,250	4,875,000
Testing	97,500	29,250	848,250	975,000
Total job cost	$1,018,750	$535,750	$11,770,500	$13,325,000
Number of units	8	6	86	
Current status	In process	Complete		
Cost per unit	$127,344	$89,292		

* Allocated on the basis of direct labor hours and machine hours used by each job.

Note that the total cost assigned to jobs in Exhibit 4 ($13,325,000) is the same as the total manufacturing cost shown in Exhibit 3. Also note that the cost per heat exchanger in Exhibit 4 is $127,344 for the Sweden job and $89,292 for Zimbabwe job. Finally, the cost per unit is different for the two jobs. Alfa Laval has already spent $127,344 per unit ($1,018,750/8) for Sweden's incomplete job as compared to $89,292 (535,750/6) for the fully completed units for the Zimbabwe job. This is because they use different materials and have different work specifications.

The basic mechanism for tracking costs is the *chart of accounts*. A chart of accounts is a list of accounts, each with a unique code to allow easy recording and tracking of costs in a computerized database. Account codes provide the capability to distinguish manufacturing

---

[9] See the modules *Measuring and Managing Indirect Costs* and *Manufacturing Overhead Allocation—Traditional and Activity Based* in this series.

costs from other functional costs (see box 2 in Exhibit 2). The chart of accounts and codes also allow costs to be traced to individual departments within the manufacturing function (box 3 of Exhibit 2) and to individual jobs and units produced (boxes 4 and 5 in Exhibit 2). The design of the chart of accounts is a key activity in the development of a cost measurement system. Appendix A discusses the logic of account codes and shows the flow of costs between accounts in greater detail.

Think Along

> How would our costing approach change if the heat exchangers in all jobs had identical specifications?

Process Costing at Robins.

If all jobs had identical specifications, there would be no reason for Alfa Laval to separately track the costs of each individual job. The cost per unit could be computed simply by dividing the total cost in each department by the total number of units produced in that department. For example, the total cost in stamping is $5,075,000 (see Exhibit 3). The total number of units worked on in stamping is 100 (8 + 6 + 86 as shown in Exhibit 4). Because all 100 units are identical and assuming they have all been stamped and transferred to assembly, the stamping cost per unit for the heat exchanger is $50,750 ($5,075,000 ÷ 100 units). The total cost per heat exchanger would be the sum of the cost expended in all three operations.

This averaging of cost across processes is essentially what happens in our second example firm, A.H. Robins. Robins's production runs are much larger than Alfa Laval's and all units in a run are identical. A single production run may produce 2,500,000 tablets or 150,000,000 bottles of cough syrup, each exactly like the others in the batch. The processing time for various products ranges from two days to five months. The major processing steps are mixing, bottling, and packaging. Exhibit 5 below graphically represents the flow of costs in a traditional process costing system.

Exhibit 5
Cost Flows in Process Costing

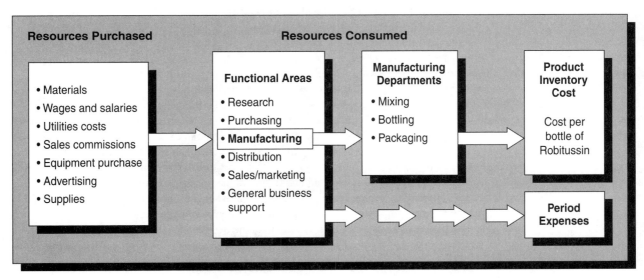

Compare Exhibit 5 with Exhibit 2, which portrays Alfa Laval's job-order costing system. In both Alfa Laval's job costing system and Robins's process costing system, the first two steps are the same—costs are traced to functional areas of the firm and then to departments within these areas. Unlike Alfa Laval's customers, however, the individuals who purchase Robins's products expect no custom features, and Robins uses identical ingredients and processes for every bottle of cough syrup.[10] Therefore, the cost per unit does not vary from customer to customer, as was the case for Alfa Laval's heat exchangers, and Robins's cost measurement system can omit the step of tracing costs to individual customers or jobs. This situation greatly simplifies the design of the cost measurement system because fewer levels of building blocks are needed. Exhibit 6 shows the cost tracking for Robins. Note that Exhibit 6 is exactly the same as Exhibit 3 for Alfa Laval, except that for Robins the processing departments are mixing, bottling, and packaging.

Exhibit 6
Product Cost in Process Costing—Robitussin Cough Syrup

	Mixing	Bottling	Packaging	Totals
Direct materials	$1,200,000	$340,000	$700,000	$2,240,000
Direct labor	50,000	40,000	80,000	170,000
Manufacturing overhead	780,000	520,000	510,000	1,810,000
Total cost	**$2,030,000**	**$900,000**	**$1,290,000**	**$4,220,000**

Assume that the total processing costs of $4,220,000 is for producing 5,000,000 bottles of Robitussin cough syrup. Because all bottles are identical, we can obtain the cost per bottle of Robitussin by dividing $4,220,000 by 5,000,000 bottles to get $ 0.844 per bottle for this batch of the cough syrup. In addition, if we assume no spoilage or shrinkage, we can divide the cost of each processing center by 5,000,000 to obtain the processing cost per bottle in each processing center. You may recall from the opening story of the module that Robins's management was concerned that the cost per bottle was increasing in the mixing department. You can see that the computed cost of $0.406 per bottle in mixing ($2,030,000 ÷ 5,000,000) is the basis for this concern.

Inventory Issues in Traditional Cost Systems.

Product cost calculations in a traditional system rarely are as simple as those described for Robins, particularly in mass production environments. Long production cycle times and inventory buffers are two key characteristics of mass production systems. Accordingly, traditional systems have large amounts of raw materials, work-in-process, and finished-goods inventories. *Work-in-process* (WIP) means that there will always be some partially completed units in each process at the end of a period. That is, some cough syrup will be boiling, some will be bottled, and some will be packaged at the end of an accounting period.

Traditional job and process costing systems deal with this problem of work-in-process inventories by computing what are called **equivalent units of output**. An equivalent unit is a way of equating partially completed and fully completed units. Assume for example that Alfa Laval had four heat exchangers that were started at the beginning of the period and that no heat exchangers were in process at the beginning. At the end of the period, two exchangers are finished, and two are half finished. We can treat the two half-finished units as one finished unit

---

[10] In fact, once the Food and Drug Administration approves a product recipe, Robins *may not* alter the formulation.

and add them to the two fully completed units. Now we can say that Alfa Laval has three equivalent finished units. Because two out of three equivalent units are complete, two-thirds of the total cost for the period represents finished goods and one-third represents the cost of work-in-process.

Think Along

What does *half finished* mean? How did we determine that the heat exchanger is half finished? How do we test whether the cost calculation makes sense?

The concept of equivalent units is based on costs to completion and not time or physical completion. A 50 percent complete unit means that one-half of the costs have been incurred. It does not mean that the unit is physically half complete or that 50 percent of the time to completion remains. These concepts of completion are important, but they are not the way accountants use the term *equivalent units*. Although these other concepts of completion may be related to cost, this is not always the case. For example, in home construction the most expensive items are finishing items (plumbing fixtures, electrical fixtures, appliances, doors, cabinets, etc.). They represent more than 35 percent of the cost but take up only 20 percent of the construction time.

To check the logic of equivalent units, let us return to the Alfa Laval example of the four heat exchangers. Assume that the total cost incurred on these heat exchangers is $450,000. Because we computed the output to be three equivalent units [2 + 2 (.5)], the cost per equivalent unit is $450,000 ÷ 3 = $150,000. Also, we know that two units are complete and have been transferred to the finished goods inventory. The transfer cost was $300,000 (2 × $150,000) and, therefore, work-in-process is $150,000. Because the $150,000 represents two (50 percent complete) units, each unit has a cost of $75,000. Completing these half-finished units, by definition, should require another $75,000 each. Thus when complete, all four heat exchangers will have the same per unit cost of $150,000.

In Robins's case, departments will have units in process from the last period (beginning work-in-process) and units in process at the end (ending work-in-process). Assume that during the current period, the mixing department started work on 5,300,000 bottles. In addition, it had 300,000 units in beginning work-in-process that were 40 percent completed last period. During the period, mixing transferred out 5,200,000 units to bottling. The remaining 400,000 units (300,000 + 5,300,000 − 5,200,000) in ending work-in-process are 70 percent complete. Exhibit 7 summarizes this data for the mixing department at Robins.

Note Pad

Compute the cost per bottle transferred from mixing to bottling.

Exhibit 7
Equivalent Units Processed by Mixing Department

	Units Produced	Completion Stage
Bottles in process at beginning of period	300,000	40% complete
Bottles started this period	5,300,000	
Number of bottles transferred to next department	5,200,000	
Bottles in process at end of period	400,000	70% complete

Exhibit 8
Equivalent Units of Output for the Mixing Department

Bottles	Equivalent Units—FIFO		Equivalent Units—Weighted Average	
Beginning WIP	180,000	(300,000 × (1−.6))	300,000	
Started and finished (5,300,000 − 400,000)	4,900,000		4,900,000	
Ending WIP	280,000	(400,000 × .7)	280,000	(400,000 × .7)
Total	**5,360,000**		**5,480,000**	

The mixing department had 300,000 bottles on which 40 percent of the cost had been incurred. This period, to complete these bottles, they incurred the other 60 percent or the equivalent of 180,000 bottles. The department started another 5,300,000 bottles, bringing the total to 5,600,000. At the end mixing has 400,000 bottles still in process that are 70 percent complete. Therefore, 4,900,000 were started and completed during the period (5,200,000 − 300,000), and the equivalent of another 280,000 complete bottles (400,000 × .70) are still in process. The mixing department, therefore, completed work on 5,360,000 equivalent bottles this period. This procedure, which separates the percentage of completion of both beginning and ending work-in-process, is called the *first-in-first-out (FIFO)* method.

A more common method for dealing with percentage of completion is called the *weighted-average method*. This method ignores the percentage of completion of the beginning work-in-process. These units are combined with the units started and completed this period. The 70 percent completed ending work is added to the 5,200,000 units transferred to yield 5,480,000 equivalent units. Exhibit 8 shows the computation of equivalent units of output for the mixing department under the two methods.[11]

Assuming the use of the weighted-average method, the information on equivalent units can be combined with the cost information from Exhibit 6 to determine the cost per equivalent unit for each cost element, as shown in Exhibit 9.

Exhibit 9
Calculation of Cost per Equivalent Unit

Cost Element	Amount	Equivalent Units Produced	Cost per Equivalent Unit
Direct materials	$1,200,000	5,480,000	$0.219
Direct labor	50,000	5,480,000	0.009
Manufacturing overhead	780,000	5,480,000	0.142
Total	**$2,030,000**		**$0.370**

Note Pad

Test your understanding of the concept of equivalent units of production by calculating the equivalent units for the bottling department. Assume the following: Beginning work-in-process inventory is 245,000 units, 30 percent complete; and ending work-in-process inventory is 240,000 units, 60 percent complete. During the current period bottling started work on another 5,200,000 units and completed and transferred 5,205,000 to packaging. (The answer is provided at the end of the module.)

---

[11] A full discussion of these methods is contained in the forthcoming advanced module on *Process Costing* in this series.

The concept of equivalent units has wide applicability. In addition to manufacturing, equivalent unit computation is relevant to service industries that have long production cycles. As college students you have may have completed two out of your four years toward a bachelor's degree at this point. From a cost perspective you are now a 50 percent equivalent finished student. Similarly, some students in your class may be full-time students, and others may be part-time students. Colleges compute their student load by adding these students through a unit called the "full-time equivalent" (FTE). Since 15 credit hours is a full-time load, two students, one with 9 credit hours and the other with 6 credit hours, will be counted as one full-time-equivalent student. In a class, however, the one equivalent student occupies two physical seats. Similarly, two students starting their junior year do not add up to one college degree. Ten half-completed planes, with only one wing attached, may be equal to five equivalent planes, but none of the planes can fly!

Key Point

> An equivalent unit is simply a way to account for two physically dissimilar units by adding together their common denominator, costs. It should not be confused with physical completion.

Weaknesses in Traditional Job Cost Systems.

Think Along

> Do the job and process cost calculations provide the information that managers at Alfa Laval and Robins need to better manage resources and to service their customers?

The costs traced to the two jobs in Exhibits 2, 3, and 4, and the cost per bottle in Exhibit 9 provide limited management insight for two main reasons.

First, total job cost and the per unit product cost of $1,018,750 and $127,344 respectively, for the Sweden job and $535,750 and $89,292 for the Zimbabwe job are neither the total cost of serving these customers nor do they represent total product cost. They are only manufacturing costs. Substantial costs incurred in other areas, such as marketing, distribution, and business support, are not included as part of the job cost. Hence the job cost calculated in this way is not the total cost of servicing a customer. The same is true for the cost per bottle of $0.37 for Robins.

Second, indirect costs account for a significant portion of the production costs in the two companies. For Alfa Laval manufacturing overhead costs account for 56 percent of total manufacturing costs (manufacturing overhead of $7,475,000/13,325,000 = .56). Single-driver allocation systems (direct labor or machine hours) used by many traditional systems to allocate indirect costs can provide a very misleading view of product cost and profitability. In addition, such single allocation systems do not provide any information about cost drivers—that is, those factors that explain what causes costs to change. Thus management has very little information to assess whether the amount of resources consumed by a customer is excessive and how to better manage these costs.

Remember how the managers in our opening story lamented the lack of information to manage costs proactively and strategically. You can begin to see why.

▲ CONTEMPORARY COST MEASUREMENT SYSTEMS

Traditional cost systems are not suited to the needs of today's competitive business environment. In particular, the advent of lean manufacturing systems, the use of Total Quality Management (TQM) techniques, and increasingly intense competition has greatly reduced the usefulness of traditional cost measurement systems.

Lean manufacturing systems use just-in-time systems and have little or no inventory. This system diminishes the usefulness of inventory valuation as a function of the cost measurement system and greatly simplifies the accounting part of the costing function because there are no work-in-process inventories and equivalent units to track.

TQM emphasizes cross-functional management of processes rather than department-based management systems. It reduces the need for responsibility accounting by departments and emphasizes instead cost management through redesign of products and processes. Cost tracking by departments does not help process management.

Finally, the competitive environment requires managers to think more strategically about how cost measurement systems can help an organization to compete effectively and to achieve its strategic goals.[12] This environment requires understanding cost drivers so costs can be managed proactively rather than reactively.

Contemporary cost measurement systems, therefore, emphasize the measurement of all costs and not just manufacturing (inventory) costs. Consistent with the process focus, contemporary cost systems use activities and operations as critical cost objects in building a cost measurement system. They also provide better information to help managers understand what drives the costs of each step in the process of developing, producing, and delivering products to customers. By analyzing costs at the detailed level of activities and operations involved in the cross-functional flow of work, these newer systems make visible how activities in one processing step may affect costs at other processing steps, thus enhancing the visibility of cost-driver relationships.

There are four important differences between traditional and contemporary approaches to cost measurement. A contemporary system:

- ▲ Provides comprehensive product cost information by including in product cost not only manufacturing costs but the costs of all activities and operations that create, produce, deliver, and support the product or service. This includes both preproduction (upstream) costs and postproduction (downstream) costs.

- ▲ Emphasizes management of the activities and operations that make up the process rather than the department that performs the work.

- ▲ Allocates indirect costs to activities/operations and from there to products rather than from responsibility centers to products.

- ▲ Supports strategic cost management by making cost driver relationships visible as opposed to emphasizing external financial reporting.

One of the more important types of contemporary cost measurement systems is an activity/operations costing system. The focus of this system is on the total product cost (not just manufacturing costs). Its key building blocks are activities and operations that constitute the major cross-functional processes.[13]

---

[12] This is one of the fourteen principles Total Quality enunciated by Edwards Deming, the leader of the quality movement.

[13] An *activity* is a series of related tasks performed by a person. An *operation* is a series of tasks performed by a piece of machinery. The distinction is not always clear, and the boundary between the two is somewhat fuzzy.

Think Along

How will Alfa Laval or Robins need to modify its cost measurement systems to adopt this new approach?

Alfa Laval—An Activity and Operations Costing View.

To convert Alfa Laval's traditional job costing system into an activity/operations costing system, we must start by developing a *process map*, which is a graphic representation of the sequence of activities/operations that must be performed to produce a heat exchanger. The heat exchangers in the two customer jobs examined earlier go through many activities and manufacturing operations. These activities involve all functional areas of the organization. Exhibit 10 is an abbreviated process map of some of the major activities/operations required by the two customer jobs.

Exhibit 11 identifies the functional area that has primary responsibility for each activity. Note that the various activities and operations involve all the functional areas and departments at Alfa Laval. Although we have kept this example simple, in practice many of the activities also cut across functional boundaries and involve several functions. A good example is drafting a contract. The legal, sales, engineering, and manufacturing departments all participate in this activity.

Each activity/operation consumes resources. The cost differences across jobs result from the fact that the various jobs require different activities and therefore consume different amounts of resources. To compute the cost of the two customer jobs, we must perform the following steps:

1. Identify activities and operations used by each job.[14]
2. Compute the costs of these activities and operations (including both direct and indirect costs).
3. Determine the cost drivers for each activity/operation.
4. Combine costs of activities that have common drivers into cost pools.
5. Assign costs to jobs based on the drivers each job consumes.
6. Determine unit product cost.

We can illustrate this six-step process using a sample of the activities identified in Exhibits 10 and 11.

1. Identify activities/operations used by jobs.

Notice that the completion of this job requires activities and operations in many areas of the organization. Substantial resources are required to support the activities performed by marketing personnel in visiting the prospective customer, by engineering personnel in developing product specifications, and by customer support personnel in the installation at the customer site. These activities are essential to complete the process of providing a heat exchanger to a customer, but traditional job-order costing systems do not treat these as part of the cost of heat exchangers. Costs of these activities must be included, however, to understand the full cost of the job. To understand why the cost of the Sweden job differs from the cost of other jobs, management needs to analyze which activities are unique to this job.

---

[14] Methods of documenting activities and computing their costs are discussed in detail in the modules *Activity-Based Management* and *Manufacturing Overhead Allocations—Traditional and Activity Based* in this series.

Exhibit 10
Abbreviated Process Map for Alfa Laval's Customer Jobs

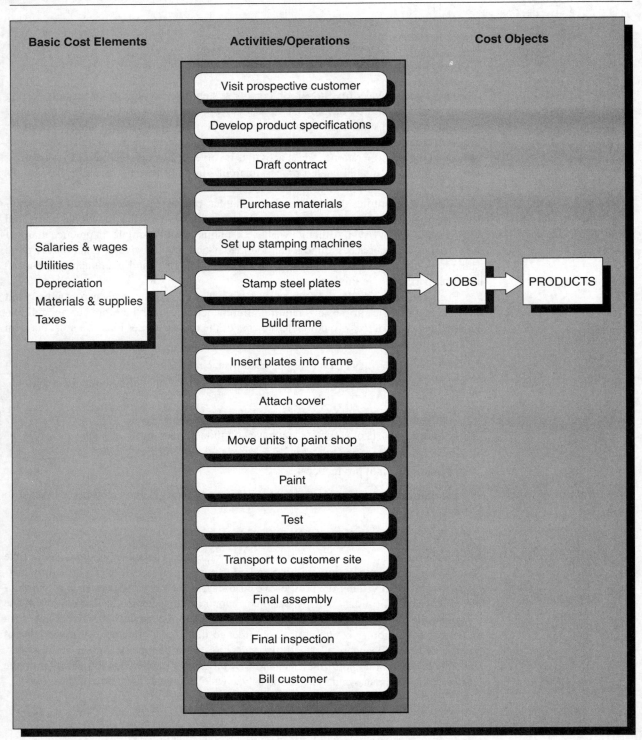

Exhibit 11
Activities/Operations for Alfa Laval's Customer Jobs

Activity or Operation in the Process	Functional Area with Primary Responsibility
Visit prospective customer	Sales and marketing
Develop product specifications	Engineering
Draft contract	Legal
Purchase materials	Purchasing
Set up stamping machines	Stamping
Stamp steel plates	Stamping
Build frame	Assembly
Insert plates into frames	Assembly
Attach cover	Assembly
Move units to paint shop	Assembly
Paint	Assembly
Test	Testing
Transport to customer site	Customer support
Final assembly	Customer support
Final inspection	Customer support
Bill customer	General administration
Other activities	Various

2. Compute the costs of the activities and operations.

Each activity uses resources such as people, materials, factory space, and other cost items. Some cost items, such as operator salaries and supplies, are traceable to particular activities and operations. Other costs, such as property taxes on buildings, are indirect and have to be allocated to activities/operations based on *resource-usage drivers* such as square feet of space required by an activity. Exhibit 12 shows the results of this analysis for Alfa Laval.[15]

Exhibit 12
Activity Costs for Heat Exchangers

Activity or Operation	Cost
Visit prospective customer	$83,600
Develop product specifications	608,000
Draft contract	270,000
Purchase materials	288,000
Set up stamping machines	1,176,000
Stamp steel plates	3,952,000
Build frame	756,000
Insert plates into frames	5,040,000
Attach cover	126,000
Move unit to paint shop	9,000
Paint	480,000
Test	770,000
Transport to customer site	910,000
Final assembly	702,000
Final inspection	504,000
Bill customer	8,400
Other activities	87,000
Total activities cost	**$15,770,000**

---

[15] How to document and obtain the cost of activities is discussed in detail in the *Activity-Based Management* module in this series.

Exhibit 13
Activity Cost per Unit of Cost Driver

Activity or Operation	Cost	Driver	Units of Driver	Cost per Unit of Driver
Visit prospective customer	$ 83,600	Number of trips	22	$3,800
Develop product specifications	608,000	Engineering hours	3,800	160
Draft contract	270,000	Legal staff hours	1,800	150
Purchase materials	288,000	Per purchase order	2,400	120
Set up stamping machines	1,176,000	Per production run	120	9,800
Stamp steel plates	3,952,000	Per machine hour	520	7,600
Build frame	756,000	Per component	420	1,800
Insert plates in frames	5,040,000	Per plate	6,300	800
Attach cover	126,000	Attachment points	2,100	60
Move to paint shop	9,000	Per unit	120	75
Paint	480,000	Surface area, sq. ft.	32,000	15
Test	770,000	Per test	275	2,800
Transport to customer site	910,000	Per trip	140	6,500
Final assembly	702,000	Per unit	120	5,850
Final inspection	504,000	Per unit	120	4,200
Bill customer	8,400	Per bill	28	300
Other activities	87,000			
Total activities cost	**$15,770,000**			

3. Determine cost drivers for each activity and operation.

The accountant must work closely with personnel in other areas of the organization to determine what causal factors increase or decrease the cost of an activity. These causal factors are referred to as "cost drivers." Identifying the cost driver for the activity "developing product specifications," for example, may require talking to design engineers, sales people, manufacturing engineers, machine operators, quality assurance, installers, service engineers, and cost analysts. The analysis may reveal that the number of engineering hours consumed is the cost driver for this activity. The next step is to divide the cost of the activity by the number of engineering hours consumed to determine the activity/operation cost per unit of the driver. This analysis is shown in Exhibit 13.

Although this type of first-level cost driver is sufficient for assigning activity costs to heat exchangers, Alfa Laval may find it useful to conduct additional levels of analysis for cost management purposes. Exhibit 13 shows that using one more engineering hour for developing product specifications increases cost by $160. To manage engineering costs, however, they need to know what causes engineering hours to go up. For example, the heat exchangers being produced for Sweden must withstand severe winter weather and operate under various climatic conditions in the plant. Accordingly, engineering personnel have to spend additional time researching how to make existing components operate under different environmental conditions. Engineering hours, therefore, are being driven by the "variety of operating conditions" under which the heat exchanger must perform.

Key Point

To manage the cost of engineering hours consumed, Alfa Laval must go beyond the obvious cost drivers and understand the deeper levels of cost drivers.

4. Create cost pools for common cost drivers.

Some cost drivers may be common to several activities. Consider, for example, the activities "final assembly" and "final inspection." The cost driver for both activities is "number

Exhibit 14
Alfa Laval—Costs Assigned to Jobs

Activity	Sweden Job WE-046-12-061-97		Zimbabwe Job SA-263-15-026-97	
	Units of Cost Driver	Cost Assigned	Units of Cost Driver	Cost Assigned
Visit prospective customer	4	$15,200	1	$3,800
Develop product specifications	1,400	224,000	300	48,000
Draft contract	18	2,700	4	600
Purchase materials	240	28,800	90	10,800
Set up stamping machines	11	107,800	3	29,400
Stamp steel plates	22	167,200	8	60,800
Build frame	38	68,400	25	45,000
Insert plates into frames	280	224,000	95	76,000
Attach cover	122	7,320	90	5,400
Move unit to paint shop	14	1,050	6	450
Paint	3,800	57,000	825	12,375
Test	18	50,400	6	16,800
Transport to customer site	0	0	2	13,000
Final assembly	0	0	6	35,100
Final inspection	0	0	6	25,200
Bill customer	0	0	1	300
Total activities cost		**$953,870**		**$383,025**

of units." To simplify calculations, the costs associated with these two activities can be combined and treated as a single cost pool for allocation purposes. Aggregating costs by common cost drivers highlight those cost drivers that account for a significant portion of costs and thus helps to focus cost management efforts on the correct variables.

5. Assign costs based on drivers.
The next step is to assign costs to jobs based on the drivers consumed. Exhibit 14 shows this analysis as well as the calculation of cost per unit for each job.

6. Determine unit product cost.
The determination of unit product cost requires adding the cost of specific materials issued for each job to the cost of each activity or operation consumed by that job and dividing by the number of equivalent completed units in that job. Exhibit 15 shows this analysis and compares it to the traditional cost analysis for these same jobs.

Exhibit 15
Comparison of Job Cost

	Sweden		Zimbabwe	
	Total Job Cost	Cost per Unit	Total Job Cost	Cost per Unit
Activity/operations view				
Materials cost	$546,000	$68,250	$282,000	$47,000
Activities cost	953,870	119,234	383,025	63,838
Total cost	$1,499,870	$187,484	$665,025	$110,838
Traditional view				
Direct materials	$546,000	$68,250	$282,000	$47,000
Direct labor	34,000	4,250	45,750	7,625
Manufacturing overhead	438,750	54,844	208,000	34,667
Total cost	**$1,018,750**	**$127,344**	**$535,750**	**$89,292**

Notice that the activity/operations costs for the two jobs ($1,499,870 for Sweden; $665,025 for Zimbabwe) is substantially greater than that derived by Alfa Laval's traditional job order system ($1,018,750 for Sweden; $535,750 for Zimbabwe).

Think Along

> Why is the cost per unit from the contemporary cost measurement system shown here different from the cost per unit determined by the traditional job-order costing system?

You may recall that the traditional cost measurement system described in Exhibits 3 and 4 includes only manufacturing costs. A contemporary activity/operations cost system traces all costs from other functional areas, such as engineering and customer support, and assigns these costs to jobs based on the usage of these activities.

Robins—An Activity and Operations Costing View.

Like Alfa Laval, Robins can use the six steps described above to make their cost system more consistent with the contemporary activity/operations-based approach. Because all the steps, with the exception of tracing costs to jobs, are the same as for Alfa Laval, we will not illustrate them again in detail. Exhibit 16 provides an example of the final numbers that Robins's contemporary cost system might produce.[16]

Think Along

> The mixing cost of a bottle of Robitussin as calculated by the activity-based analysis is $0.28. Why is this value different from the mixing cost per bottle of $0.37 shown in Exhibit 9?

The main difference between the costs shown in Exhibit 9 and those shown below (Exhibit 16) is due to the allocation of manufacturing overhead costs. In a traditional system all manufacturing overhead is first charged to the three processing centers and then to products. In an activity-based system, the overhead costs are charged first to activities and then to products.[17]

Also note that Robins's new cost system shown in Exhibit 16, provides an analysis of costs by traditional categories as well as by activities/operations and by cost drivers. This "kaleidoscopic view" of costs allows Robins to see the $2.05 cost per bottle of Robitussin cough syrup in many ways. The first is by type of resources consumed—that is, materials, wages, supplies, utilities, equipment, and so on. Next it also shows cost by activities. Finally, Robins can also see costs by drivers.

---

[16] Exhibit 16 has been adapted from an article on Teva Pharmaceutical Industries Ltd., which describes its experience in developing an activity-based cost system. The article supports our hypothetical example by showing how in the real world a company in the same business as Robins can use an activity/operations costing system. See Robert Kaplan, Dan Weiss and Eyal Dinesh, "Transfer Pricing with ABC," *Management Accounting*, May 1997, pp. 20–28.

[17] For a detailed discussion of why differences in allocation systems result in different cost assignments, see the module *Manufacturing Overhead Allocation: Traditional and Activity Based* in this series.

Exhibit 16
Sample Cost Breakdown for Robitussin Using a Contemporary Cost System

Classification	Cost	Classification	Cost
By Resources:		**By Activities:**	
Materials	$0.42	Develop customer relations	$.04
Labor	0.03	Process orders	.02
Manufacturing overhead		New product development	.34
Supplies	0.02	Purchase chemicals	.06
Utilities	0.06	Secure storage	.04
Wages	0.14	Issue chemicals to production	.02
Equipment	0.10	Print cartons	.09
Other	0.02	Mixing	.28
Subtotal	0.34	Bottling	.23
		Packaging	.35
Other costs		Quality assurance	.06
Shipping supplies	0.04	Equipment maintenance	.25
Utilities	0.05	Move to storage	.02
Salaries	0.90	Distribution	.03
Equipment	0.07	Billing	.22
Other	0.20	**Total**	**$2.05**
Subtotal	1.26		
Total	**$2.05**		

Classification	Cost
By Cost Drivers:	
Customer calls	$.07
Purchase orders	.03
Engineering hours	.31
Material moves, secured	.11
Material moves, unsecured	.02
Production runs	.35
Number of colors	.13
Machine hours	.67
Number of bottles	.33
Number of bills	.03
Total	**$2.05**

Comparison of Traditional and Contemporary Cost Systems.

Traditional and contemporary cost measurement systems are built on fundamentally different conceptual foundations. A traditional cost system uses responsibility centers (commonly defined as departments or functional areas of the firm) as a key cost object in tracking cost flows. A contemporary cost system uses activities/operations as intermediate cost objects to trace costs to final cost objects. It assigns costs to final cost objects based on cost drivers and provides multiple views of costs—by resources consumed, by activities consumed, and by drivers consumed. The contemporary approach facilitates

Exhibit 17
Cost Flow Differences between Traditional (top) and Contemporary (bottom) Cost Systems

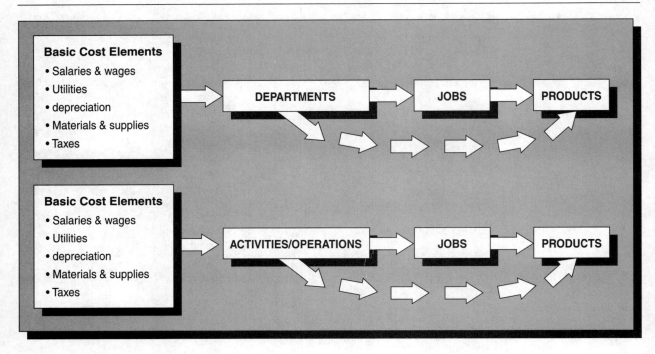

cost management by making these various causal relationships visible to managers. Exhibit 17 shows the differences in cost flows between these two approaches.

Another important difference is that the two systems define product costs differently. Exhibit 18 below shows this difference. A traditional system, the shaded portion of Exhibit 18, includes only manufacturing and manufacturing support costs in product costs. A contemporary system includes, in addition, the cost of all traceable activities in computing per unit product cost. Some costs, such as management training or the costs of operating corporate headquarters, are so distant from any specific product that both types of systems may choose not to trace them to products. However, by including these other costs, a contemporary cost system enhances the visibility of nonmanufacturing costs and provides a more comprehensive view of a job's profitability.

This difference between the two approaches represents the difference between generally accepted accounting principles (GAAP) and managerial use of accounting data. GAAP has a more restrictive definition of what can be included in product cost. An activity-based system allows many more costs to be directly identified with products. It is interesting to see whether GAAP rules will change to allow more costs to be part of product cost.[18]

A third difference between the two systems is that activity-based systems focus attention on the process of work rather than on who does the work. The contemporary system tells Alfa Laval's management that the most expensive activities are inserting plates in frames, and stamping steel plates.

---

[18] It is interesting to note that the income tax treatment is also different from GAAP. Many other costs, such as interest, treated as an expense by GAAP must be capitalized in determining product costs for tax reporting.

Exhibit 18
Product Cost Buildup—Traditional and Contemporary

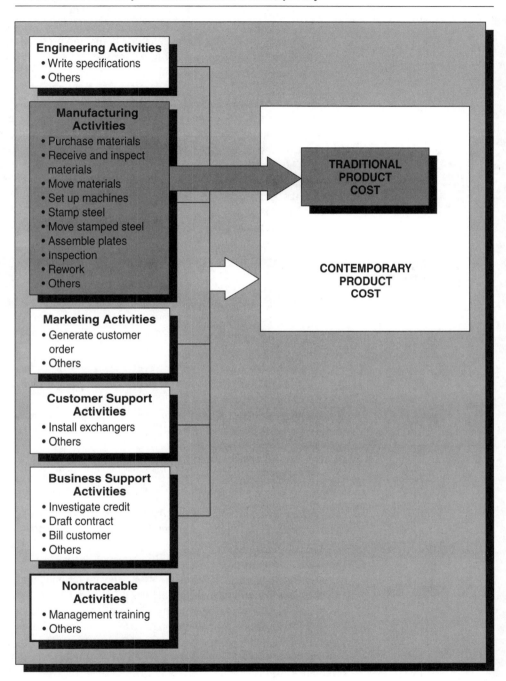

Finally, the contemporary system provides comprehensive product cost information by functions, resources, activities, and cost drivers. The information on cost drivers is particularly useful in managing and redesigning work processes. For example, the data in

Exhibit 16 facilitates effective cost management in several ways. The resource breakdown shows Robins that its single largest cost category is general and administrative salaries, which total roughly 44 percent of the total product cost of $2.05. The activity analysis shows packaging and new-product development are the two costliest activities. Finally, analysis of costs by drivers shows machine hours and production runs are the most significant cost drivers for Robins, accounting for 65% of the product cost for Robitussin. The cost management strategy for Robins should be to reduce materials price and usage, search for ways to better perform new product development and packaging activities, and reduce the number of machine hours used if possible.

Although the contemporary cost measurement system expands the definition of costs, it is still not a complete picture of all costs incurred to serve a customer. What a customer pays for Robitussin includes costs incurred by firms that provide or receive services from Robins. They are part of the value chain of suppliers and dealers that enable the cough syrup to get to the final consumer. Few cost measurement systems in use today track such costs, partly because of the practical problems associated with analyzing costs incurred by different organizations. However, a large part of the reason is a lack of trust that makes organizations reluctant to share cost information with others.

Key Point

> Although many costs are traceable to products, under current GAAP many such costs cannot be included as inventory cost on the balance sheet. In an activity/operations costing system, each discrete *activity* and each *manufacturing operation* become cost objects. The product cost includes many activities and operations that are traceable to products.

▲ ATTRIBUTES OF A COST MEASUREMENT SYSTEM

A well-designed cost measurement system must have desirable technical, behavioral, and cultural attributes.

Technical Attributes.

A cost measurement system should improve the quality of management decisions and enhance their process understanding to facilitate process management.

Decision relevance.

For a cost system to provide information relevant to management's decisions, cost objects must be related to the strategic objectives of quality, cost, and time. For example, cost measurement systems must help managers understand the costs associated with providing existing levels of quality and estimate costs of adding features desired by their customers. The following quote from a manager at Hewlett-Packard's circuit board assembly plant in Palo Alto, California, reflects the expectations of managers with regard to their cost measurement systems.

> We expect our cost system to do more than just allocate costs and produce reports. We need to know what drives these costs. We want the cost system to talk to our design engineers so they can carry their understanding of costs into product designs that are cost-effective to produce.

Note that at Hewlett-Packard the test of a good system is its ability to improve product design decisions. The cost system aids engineers in designing better products by showing them how design decisions drive product costs. We have seen in this module that traditional systems are of little help in proactively managing costs, since they focus on departments and not on cost drivers. The contemporary approach's focus on cost drivers improves decisions about where to spend managerial time and what areas to focus on.

Process understanding.

A good cost measurement system must help managers to understand their work processes and the economic impact of activities or operations that reduce quality, increase cost, or cause delays. This feature is a major strength of the contemporary cost systems. Their primary focus is work operations and activities. As we have seen, their starting point is a process map (Exhibit 10). Contemporary systems can readily extend the analysis to include all value chain activities, thereby providing a more comprehensive process view than a system constrained by the departmental boundaries of a single organization. Finally, the cost impact of manufacturing and innovation cycle time are not made visible by traditional systems. By emphasizing costs across all steps in a process, a contemporary cost measurement system can reveal which activities or operations cause delays and thus cause cost increases.

Behavioral Attributes.

Cost measurement systems can affect behavior of people in organizations in many ways. The selection of cost objects can be a particularly important means of changing behavior in organizations because a cost object makes the selected variable *visible*, *focuses attention*, and *communicates* managerial intent. When selected carelessly, the cost system can lead to dysfunctional behaviors.

Consider the use of DRGs as cost objects by hospitals. Many industry observers claim that this shift has made hospitals play games to provide proper health care to patients. Hospitals sometimes discharge and then readmit patients under a different DRG to complete the treatment for a single episode or ailment when a patient's length of stays exceeds that permitted by a DRG. Similarly, state colleges measure costs based on equivalent full-time students. Some critics charge that this method of measuring and funding state colleges has led to overcrowding in the classroom.

Another way in which cost measurement systems can change behaviors is through highlighting cost drivers. Cost driver analysis can focus attention on managing the right variables and can also help to communicate efficient and better design rules and practices. As the Hewlett-Packard quote points out, many world-class organizations use their cost measurement system to communicate with design engineers about how to develop better and more cost-effective product and process designs.[19] They do this by penalizing designs that consume more of critical cost drivers. This approach forces designers to explicitly consider cost as an important variable in putting features and functions into products and in choosing the processes to produce and deliver these products.[20]

---

[19] For example, see D. Berlant, R. Browning, and G. Foster, "How Hewlett-Packard Gets Numbers It Can Trust," *Harvard Business Review*, Jan-Feb 1990, pp. 178–183 and T. Hiromoto, "Another Hidden Edge—Japanese Management Accounting," *Harvard Business Review*, July-Aug 1988, pp. 22–26.

[20] The *Target Costing* module in this series discusses cost management in the product design phase in greater detail.

A well-designed cost measurement system uses the selection of cost objects and cost measurement rules as an opportunity to reinforce behaviors that lead to the accomplishment of strategic objectives. When properly selected, that cost object will make visible customer requirements throughout the organization, reduce product costs, and decrease cycle time for manufacturing, innovation, or delivery.

Cultural Attributes.

A cost measurement system both reflects and reinforces an organization's culture. In an organization where finding fault and laying blaming are a pervasive *mind-set*, the cost measurement system becomes a tool toward that end. Traditional systems, in general, are more susceptible to this because they are responsibility-focused, and therefore encourage the tendency to assign blame. They reinforce the role of the accountant as a corporate cop. On the other hand, activity systems have a process focus. They encourage improving processes by looking for underlying causes of changes in costs. By focusing on cost drivers and cross-functional processes, activity-based cost measurement systems transform the role of an accountant from a cop to a business advisor.[21] Management accountants become symbols and actors that help to create and foster a healthy organization culture.

The selection of cost objects can send symbolic messages in an organization. An organization that uses cost objects related solely to profitability and efficiency sends a message that it cares only for its own well-being. A corporation that measures costs for cost objects such as the environment, social activities, and human resource development can use these cost objects as powerful symbols to say that it is socially responsible and cares about its people and the environment.

▲ LESSONS LEARNED

- ▲ A cost measurement system is part of a strategic management accounting system that helps an organization to meet its strategic objectives of quality, cost, and time.
- ▲ A cost measurement system is like a building process that transforms raw data about resource purchases into useful information about resources consumed.
- ▲ The design of a cost measurement system involves selecting the right cost objects, establishing a chart of accounts and codes to track cost flows, and establishing rules for allocating the cost of shared resources.
- ▲ The type of cost measurement system an organization uses typically reflects the nature of products or services it produces and the production methods it uses.
- ▲ Firms that fabricate, assemble products from parts, or provide personal services using mass production techniques typically use job-order or batch costing. Firms using mass production methods in extractive and process industries typically use process costing.
- ▲ Traditional job and process cost systems trace costs first to departments (responsibility units) and from there to units produced.

---

[21] For an extended discussion of these two roles of accountants, see *The Organizational Role of the Management Accountants* module in this series.

▲ Firms using lean production methods typically use activity/operations costing systems. These contemporary cost systems trace costs first to activities and operations and then to units produced.

▲ An activity/operations costing system provides more comprehensive product cost data and makes cost drivers visible to managers.

▲ A well-designed cost measurement system improves decisions and facilitates process management by providing data on the cost of outputs produced, the cost of the processes (activities) used, and the underlying causal relationships (drivers) that cause costs to change. A good cost system encourages behaviors consistent with strategic objectives and creates mindsets and values that create a healthy and positive organizational culture.

Solution to Notepad p. CMS–15.
Equivalent Units in Bottling

Bottles	Equivalent Units—Weighted Average		Equivalent Units—FIFO	
Beginning WIP	245,000		171,500	(245,000 × (1−.3))
Started and finished (5,205,000 − 245,000)	4,960,000		4,960,000	
Ending WIP	144,000	(240,000 × .6)	144,000	(240,000 × .6)
Total	**5,349,000**		**5,275,500**	

APPENDIX

▲ COST TRACKING—TECHNICAL ISSUES

This appendix explains how a *chart of accounts* and *account codes* allow Alfa Laval to generate the job cost data shown in Exhibits 3 and 4. Before you read on, it may be useful for you to review once more the job costs identified in these exhibits.

Cost Flows and the Chart of Accounts.

A *chart of accounts* is a series of general ledger accounts that record the resources acquired and the resources used by an organization. Consider the information in Exhibits 3 and 4. We know that during the current period, Alfa Laval used materials, labor, machinery, utilities, supplies, and so on to produce heat exchangers. We also know that some of the work was complete and was transferred to customers and some work is still in process. The resources used during the current period were acquired in prior periods (materials) or during the current period (employee wages).

To understand the flow of costs during the current period, we must gather and record data pertaining to resource acquisition and use. Exhibit 19 summarizes this data for Alfa Laval.

The data for Exhibit 19 comes from various source documents. For example, purchase orders, receipts, and invoices paid are documents generated when materials are purchased. A material requisition slip is the source document that identifies the type of material requested, who requested it, and for what job.

Exhibit 20 below uses T-accounts to show how Alfa Laval records the information from source documents into various accounts. The letters a to l correspond to the items listed in Exhibit 19.

Can you reconcile these numbers with the numbers shown in Exhibits 3 and 4 of the module?

The top part of Exhibit 20 shows the source documents. We know from looking at invoices that we purchased $12,800,000 of materials this period. The material requisition slips tell us that $4,700,000 worth of materials were issued to departments for specific jobs. The departmental amounts are the same as those in Exhibit 3. In addition, another $1,600,000 in materials was issued but could not be identified with specific jobs and is initially charged to the manufacturing overhead account. Alfa Laval started the period with a beginning materials inventory of $3,000,000; after the new purchases and uses, it has an ending inventory balance of $9,500,000.

In each department a work-in-process account combines the materials, labor, and other manufacturing costs for production during a period. Because not all work is completed within the accounting period, the work-in-process accounts also start with a beginning and ending balance. As work is completed, the cost of completed jobs is transferred from work-in-process of a preceding department to the work-in-process of the succeeding department. The last department, assembly, transfers its completed items to the Finished Goods Inventory account.[22] Finally, when goods are shipped to customers, we record the sales revenue and move the cost of that job from the Finished Goods Inventory account to

---

[22] Realistically, Alfa Laval will have little or no finished goods inventory, due to the nature of its product. The heat exchangers are all done to order, and final assembly occurs at the customer's location.

Exhibit 19
Alfa Laval—Data on Resources Purchased and Used

Item	Description
a.	Purchase of materials, $12,800,000.
b.	Direct materials requisitioned by production departments: stamping $3,200,000; assembly $1,200,000; testing $300,000.
c.	Indirect materials consumed, $1,600,000.
d.	Direct labor recorded: stamping $250,000; assembly $750,000; testing $150,000.
e.	Indirect labor recorded, $1,200,000.
f.	Actual manufacturing overhead costs incurred, including $400,000 in depreciation on manufacturing equipment and $4,400,000 in other items.
g.	Overhead applied to production departments at rate of $6.50 per direct labor dollar.
h.	Movement of jobs from stamping to assembly, $8,000,000.
i.	Movement of jobs from assembly to testing, $14,000,000.
j.	Completion of jobs, $18,000,000.
k.	Delivery of completed units to customer sites, cost of goods sold recorded.
l.	$19,500,000. Sales revenue and accounts receivable recorded, $28,000,000; general and administrative expenses recorded, $6,550,000.

Exhibit 20
Alfa Laval—Cost Flows and Source Documents

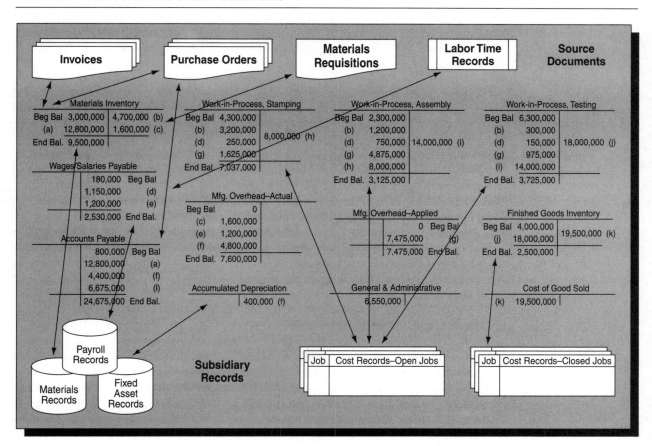

Cost of Goods Sold. General & Administrative expenses of $6,550,000 are not treated as part of product cost and are expensed at the end of the period when financial statements are prepared.

Before any department transfers out a job, it must allocate a portion of the indirect manufacturing costs to that job. In a traditional job-order costing system, the actual overhead costs are first traced to departments and then assigned to jobs using predetermined departmental or plantwide overhead rates. A predetermined rate is an estimate based on the total budgeted dollars of overhead for the year divided by a budgeted allocation base such as machine hours, labor hours, or labor dollars. Because a detailed discussion of overhead allocation is beyond the scope of this module, we will simply use a plantwide rate to illustrate the cost flows.

Assume that Alfa Laval's budget calls for total labor cost of $1,170,000 and estimated overhead costs of $7,600,000. At the beginning of the accounting period, the company would calculate an overhead application rate as follows:

$$\text{Overhead Rate} = \frac{7,600,000}{1,170,000} = \$6.50 \text{ (rounded) per direct labor dollar}$$

Notice in Exhibit 20 that the overhead cost assigned to each department is 6.5 times the direct labor cost for that department. At the end of any given period, there is a difference between overhead costs incurred and overhead costs charged to jobs. This difference is called *under-* or *overapplied overhead* and is charged to the Cost of Goods Sold account at the end of the period.

Finally, note that the bottom part of Exhibit 20 shows the subsidiary records that support the cost tracking. For instance, payroll records for employees support labor cost tracking. Individual job cost sheets allow separation of material, labor, and overhead costs by jobs.

Think Along

How would the accounts used be different in a contemporary cost measurement system?

Account Codes.

For a firm to benefit from an activity-based approach, the accounting system must capture costs not just by departments and jobs but also by activities and operations. These systems require a new set of accounts and account codes.

Account codes are the technical mechanism that permits organizations to track costs in a variety of ways. An account code is a number assigned to an account. Each number codes a particular field of data that is of interest to the users of the system. For example, Exhibit 3 tells us that during the current period the three manufacturing departments used $4,700,000 in direct manufacturing materials. Also, we know that of this amount $3,200,000 went to the stamping department. Exhibit 4 tells us that the stamping department used $384,000 out of the $3,200,000 in materials on the Swedish job.

Clearly, Alfa Laval's accounting system must be capable of tracking all expenditures by type, function, cost center, and job. In addition, because materials purchased exceed materials used, any remaining materials have to be shown on the balance sheet as an asset. Therefore, the system must also distinguish between expenditures that create assets and categorize the asset as current or noncurrent. In database terminology the five items of interest about the expenditure for materials (type, function, cost center, job, and balance sheet classification) are called "fields." In an accounting database, the fields are coded with a single- or double-digit number. For example, direct materials may be account number 1152137. The explanation for each digit is as follows: 1 = asset, 1 = current asset, 5 = materials, 2 = manufacturing, 1 = stamping department, and 37 = Swedish job. If we want to know the total cost in stamping, the database needs to add all expenditures charged to accounts that have 21 as the fourth and fifth digit. Similarly, to get the cost of the Sweden job, we must sort all expenditures that have a 37 as their sixth and seventh digits.

In practice, account codes and the database programs that handle cost tracking are quite complex. The account codes must be flexible enough to allow for both future expansion and any special analysis management may request. Many organizations do not think far enough ahead when they establish their chart of accounts and find that their computer systems cannot code data by certain cost objects because they "have run out of digits." This problem is not trivial if you consider that the so-called millennium bug (the inability of computer programs to handle the two-digit year change from year 1999 to 2000) has cost billions of dollars to fix.

Because most traditional accounting systems track costs by responsibility centers or departments, these systems do not easily provide activity/operations costs. Firms seeking to obtain activity costs often resort to one-time special cost studies to obtain this data. We believe that in the long run, this approach is costly. If possible, the system should be modified to provide an additional field for activity/operations coding of raw data.

One solution, for organizations that can afford it, is to use software packages called enterprise resource planning (ERP) programs to track cost flows.[23] These packages can track resources in various ways. For example, sorting all employees by a certain field will tell us the salary cost for a functional area such as manufacturing or engineering. Most of these software packages are adding modules that allow organizations to organize and sort data by activities and operations. This feature will make it easier for organizations to move from traditional to contemporary cost systems in the future.

---

[23] Some major ERP software packages/providers are BANYAN, PEOPLESOFT, ORACLE, and SAP.

▲ COMMON TERMS*

Activity   The series of related tasks that are part of work performed in an organization. It represents what is done such as the several things needed to load a truck with goods to be shipped, or responding to a customer complaint. (See Process diagram.)

Activity-Based Costing (ABC)   A method of costing in which activities are the primary cost objects. ABC measures cost and performance of activities and assigns the costs of those activities to other cost objects, such as products or customers, based on their use of activities.

Allocation   The apportionment or distribution of a common cost between two or more cost objects. In accounting, allocation is usually a way of assigning a cost between cost objects (products, departments or processes) that share that common cost. An allocation involves dividing the cost needed to allocate by some physical quantity (ideally a cost driver).

Benchmarking   The process of investigating and identifying "best practices" and using them as a standard to improve one's own processes and activities.

Budget   A quantitative plan of action that helps an organization coordinate resource inflows and outflows for a specific time period. Budgets are usually financial but may also include nonfinancial operating information.

Capacity   The physical facilities, personnel, supplier contacts, and processes necessary to meet the product or service needs of customers.

Competitive Analysis   Tools that enable companies to quantify how performance and costs compare against competitors, understand why performance and costs are different, and apply that insight to strengthen competitive responses and implement proactive plans.

Continuous Improvement   A program to improve the strategic variables of quality, cost or time in small incremental steps on a continuous basis.

Cost   A monetary measure of the resources consumed by a product, service, function, or activity. It also refers to the price paid for acquiring a product or service.

Cost Driver   An event or factor that has a systematic relationship to a particular type of cost and causes that cost to be incurred.

Cost Management   The systematic analysis of cost drivers for the purpose of understanding how to reduce or maintain costs.

Cost Object   Any item (activity, customer, project, work unit, product, channel, or service) for which a measurement of cost is desired.

Culture   The collective values, beliefs, ethics, and mindsets of the members of an organization, clan, or society which is subconsciously used to interpret events and take action. It is often called the collective programming of the subconscious mind.

Extended Enterprise   The extended enterprise includes an organization's customers, suppliers, dealers, and recyclers. It captures the interdependencies across these separate organizations. It is also referred to as the value chain.

Fixed Cost   A cost element that does not vary with changes in production volume in the short-run. The property taxes on a factory building is an example of a fixed production cost.

---

* The list of common terms for all modules is available online at www.mhhe.com/modules.

Incremental Cost   1. The cost associated with increasing the output of an activity or project above some base level. 2. The additional cost associated with selecting one economic or business alternative over another, such as difference between working overtime or subcontracting the work.

Indirect Costs   Costs that are not directly assignable or traceable to a cost object.

Life-Cycle Costs   Accumulation of costs for activities that occur over the entire life cycle of a product from inception to abandonment.

Process   A series of linked activities that perform a specific objective. A process has a beginning, an end, and clearly identified inputs and outputs.

Process

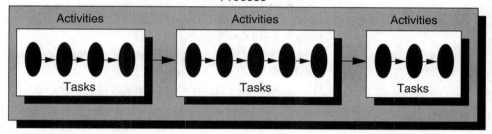

Quality   A customer's total experience with a product or service. It includes features and the performance dimensions of those features such as reliability, usability, safety, and repairability.

Strategy   The way that an organization positions and differentiates itself from its competitors. Positioning refers to the selection of target customers. Distinctions typically are made on the dimensions of quality, cost, and time.

Time   The time it takes a firm to develop and produce new products or to provide existing products when customers need them.

Value Chain   (See Extended Enterprise.)

Variable Cost   A cost element that varies directly and proportionately with changes in production volume.

▲ PROBLEMS AND CASES—INTRODUCTORY LEVEL

1. Self-test Questions.

a. What are the four components of a strategic management accounting system?

b. What are the three primary building blocks of a cost measurement system?

c. How should an organization determine what cost objects it needs?

d. What is cost allocation?

e. How does responsibility accounting differ from more modern cost measurement systems?

f. How is *product cost* defined for financial-reporting purposes?

g. Give examples of some cost items that are not part of product cost using the financial-reporting definition, but which would be included in product cost in a modern cost measurement system.

h. Give several examples of cost items that would be classified as period costs in a traditional cost measurement system.

i. Give several examples of firms that would use job-order costing.

j. What level of building blocks does a job-order costing system use that would not be found in a process costing system?

k. Describe the journal entries that are used to record manufacturing costs in a traditional job-order costing system.

l. Give several examples of firms that would use process costing.

m. What is an equivalent unit of production?

n. Why is inventory valuation less important in the cost measurement systems of firms that use modern manufacturing techniques?

o. Explain in your own words the three major differences between modern and traditional cost measurement systems.

p. What is a process map?

q. Name and explain the six steps involved in determining product cost in a modern cost measurement system.

r. What is a cost driver?

s. Exhibit 17 of the module shows some activity costs that are not traced to products. Why is this?

t. Explain why a modern cost measurement system provides superior process understanding.

u. Give an example of the behavioral impact of different definitions of cost objects.

v. What mindset does traditional responsibility accounting foster?

Exercises, Problems, and Cases.

2. For each of the firms described below, identify a strategic decision related to each leg of the strategic triangle (quality, cost, time). For each decision identified, what cost objects should be defined in the firm's CMS?

a. Heartthrob, Inc., which manufactures two kinds of heart monitors, including one for fitness enthusiasts to wear while working out and another for people at risk for heart attacks.

b. Mug Shots, Inc., produces insulated coffee mugs for Starbucks Coffee and Barnes & Noble Bookstores, and also produces a line of mugs with company logos on special order for organizations to use for promotional purposes.

c. TrashMasters, Inc., makes plastic trash bags using a process that includes the steps of mixing the plastic compounds, extruding sheets of plastic, and forming the sheets into bags.

d. Provident Beneficial Insurance Co. sells life insurance, homeowners' insurance, and car insurance to individuals and corporations.

3. You are conducting a continuing education course for financial managers. At the first session you presented the diagrams shown in Exhibits 2, 5, and 17 of the module, and described the basic differences between traditional job order and process costing and contemporary cost measurement systems. Two financial managers from a local hospital are debating whether the hospital should use job-order costing or process costing. A third individual comments that because hospitals are labor-intensive service organizations, the only kind of cost measurement system they should consider is an activity-based system. How will you (diplomatically) resolve this issue? (Hint: Consider the technical, behavioral, and cultural attributes of the cost measurement systems.)

4. Consider the following list of cost items:
- ▲ Production workers' wages.
- ▲ Salaries of product design engineers.
- ▲ The salary of an accountant at corporate headquarters.
- ▲ The president's salary.
- ▲ Salaries of customer sales representatives.
- ▲ Utilities for the factory.
- ▲ Commissions paid to sales staff.
- ▲ Supplies and salaries related to maintaining records for a major customer who orders parts just-in-time and is billed monthly.

Required:
a. For each item, indicate whether it would be considered part of product cost by a traditional cost measurement system.
b. For each item, indicate whether it would be considered part of product cost by a contemporary cost measurement system.

5. Fragonard Perfume Company in Paris produces two lines of perfumes. One is a generic brand sold to tourists. The other product line is sold to exclusive name-brand retail outlets at a high markup. The resources consumed by the firm include space in Paris for a production facility and sales room, employees and equipment there, and farming costs for fields of flowers and other ingredients grown in the south of France. Among the Paris employees is a blender, referred to in the trade as a "nose," who custom blends the ingredients at a large pigeonhole desk called the "organ." A major cost item is insurance on the "nose," since only 30 individuals in the world are qualified to perform this function.

Required:
a. Prepare a listing of the main cost elements Fragonard will record and indicate how each would be classified in a traditional cost measurement system (direct materials, direct labor, indirect manufacturing costs [overhead], or nonmanufacturing costs).

b. Develop a set of account codes that Fragonard could use to record these costs. Design your codes to allow the firm to analyze costs by the nature of the resources consumed and by activities performed.

c. Of the cost elements your account codes will track, which might differ across the two types of perfume?

6. The University of Southern Iowa encourages faculty to submit proposals for research grants to various external foundations and government agencies. The university's Office of Grants and Research assists faculty in preparing and submitting proposals, and Campus Computing Services provides data entry and analysis support. Some faculty members in the chemistry department are preparing a proposal for a research project. They estimate that the direct costs associated with the project will be as follows:

Cost Item	Amount
Faculty summer support	$8,000
Graduate student stipend	4,500
Travel	1,500
Total	**$14,000**

The university requires that researchers include in their grant budgets a request for funding to recover the cost of operating the Office of Grants and Research. Each year the university calculates an indirect cost rate based on budgeted expenses for the department and the total dollar of grants it expects faculty will receive during the year. For this year the total departmental budget is $3,600,000. This amount includes $2,400,000 in general operating expenses and $1,200,000 for data entry services. Faculty members are expected to receive grants totaling $8,000,000 during the year. The university uses a traditional job-order costing system that charges indirect costs to jobs based on a predetermined rate.

Required:

a. Based on this year's budget, what will be the indirect cost rate?

b. What amount of indirect costs will be charged to the research proposal? What is the total amount the researchers must request?

c. The researchers have learned that the agency to which they plan to submit the grant proposal will reimburse indirect costs only in amounts up to 35 percent of a project's direct costs. Assume you are the university's finance director, and the chemistry professors have come to you for help. How can you help them?

d. If the researchers are not able to recover all of the indirect costs from the grant, how will these costs be covered? What cultural values are relevant to this situation?

7. A small print shop currently has two jobs in process—an elementary school textbook and a children's craft book. Both books sell for $9 per unit, and both jobs are for 2,000 books. The production of a book involves several steps. After the material is received from the author, the design department performs the preliminary activities of copyediting and typesetting. Next the book goes to printing and finally to the assembly department, which completes the process of assembling the book and attaching the binding. The two books are similar in the resources they require for design and printing. Assembly is considerably more complex for the craft book because of special design features and the need to withstand hard use. Materials requisitions and payroll records provide the following information about costs incurred on the two jobs.

	Text	Craft
Design		
Materials	800	800
Labor	144	144
Printing		
Materials	440	440
Labor	80	80
Assembly		
Materials	275	280
Labor	1,440	1,680

Labor time cards indicate that the more highly skilled workers who assembled the craft book were paid, on average, $12 per hour rather than the normal wage of $8 per hour paid to all other workers. The company applies manufacturing overhead to jobs based on a predetermined overhead rate, calculated at the beginning of the year based on budgeted spending for labor and overhead. This year's budget called for 20,000 direct labor hours, at a total cost of $180,000. Budgeted spending for overhead items was $450,000.

Required:

a. Assume the firm uses direct labor hours to apply overhead. Calculate the overhead rate and the amount of overhead applied to each job.

b. Assume the firm uses direct labor dollars as the basis for assigning overhead. Calculate the overhead rate and the amount of overhead applied to each job.

c. For each job, calculate the cost per book and the total cost for the job using each of the two overhead allocations you calculated in questions (a) and (b). Which job is more profitable?

d. Based on your calculations, what behavioral problems might arise due to the choice of an overhead allocation basis?

e. How can the choice of an overhead allocation rate affect the firm's pursuit of its strategic goals?

8. Gloria Lauren, Inc., is a couture dress company. It has three production departments—design, cutting, and sewing. The accounting system provides the following balances in the company's general ledger as of May 1.

Account No.	Description	Beginning Balance
18000	Fabric	$6,000
12000	Supplies Inventory	380
14300	Work-in-Process—Design	8,500
14500	Work-in-Process—Cutting	7,200
14700	Work-in-Process—Sewing	9,400
15000	Overhead—Applied	0
16000	Overhead—Actual	0
18000	Finished Goods Inventory	11,500
42000	Cost of Goods Sold	0
45000	General and Administrative Expenses	0
50000	Sales Revenue	0
19000	Accounts Receivable	6,500
21000	Wages and Salaries Payable	3,500
24000	Accounts Payable	8,000

Required:

a. Set up T-accounts and show how Gloria would record the following transactions/ events for the month of May. Be sure to show the beginning and ending balance for each T-account.

    i. Fabric was purchased at a cost of $1,300.

    ii. The cutting department began work on job number 98-5-761 and requisitioned fabric costing $450.

    iii. Payroll records show the following amounts were paid to employees during the month: designers, $15,000; cutters, $4,200; sewers, $6,500. The production supervisor was paid $3,000. Marketing department salaries for the month totaled $8,200; the president was paid $12,000; and the bookkeeper was paid $2,300

    iv. Supplies consumed during May, $220.

    v. Other expenses during the month were miscellaneous overhead items, $13,500, and various general and administrative expenses of $5,500.

    vi. Overhead was applied to each department at a rate of $.60 per direct labor dollar.

    vii. Jobs with $2,800 in costs were transferred from the cutting department to the sewing department.

    viii. The sewing department completed jobs with costs of $3,800. These were moved to the finished goods storage area.

    ix. Jobs with costs of $9,000 were shipped to customers. The customers were billed $23,000.

b. Determine the amount of costs that Gloria should classify as direct materials, direct labor, indirect materials, overhead, and nonmanufacturing costs.

c. A student from a local college has been hired as a summer intern. As you are explaining the account codes, the intern suggests that, since all account numbers have zeros in the last two places, it would make sense to shorten the codes, to speed up data entry and reduce the potential for errors. How do you respond to this suggestion?

9. Jack Biddle and Jeff Greene have started a business assembling disk drives. During their first month of operation, they incurred costs of $4,365 and completely assembled 85 units. In addition, they had 40 units partially assembled at the end of the month.

Required:

Assuming the ending inventory is 30 percent assembled, what is the cost per equivalent unit for the month?

10. Jen and Mary's is a small firm that produces flavored ice tea and similar drinks using only environmentally friendly ingredients and processes. The production process has two departments, processing and bottling. Tea is bottled after it is completely processed. There was no beginning or ending inventory in the bottling activity this year.

At the beginning of 1997, Jen and Mary had 22,000 gallons of kiwi-pomegranate tea in processing. Jen estimates this beginning inventory was 60 percent complete at that time for this activity. During the year processing started on 148,500 additional gallons. By the end of the year, 152,000 gallons were completely through processing. Jen believes the tea in the processing activity at the end of the year was 30 percent complete.

Jen and Mary incurred the following production costs during the year:

Cost Item	Amount
Juices and teas	$7,500
Purified water	5,000
Bottles and cases	15,200
Processing labor	24,000
Bottling labor	18,000
Depreciation and other equipment costs—processing	27,000
Depreciation and other equipment costs—bottling	10,000
Occupancy cost of plant	15,000

Processing uses 3,000 square feet of the plant space; bottling uses 1,500 square feet. In addition to these costs, Jen and Mary also incurred marketing expenses of $30,400 and administrative expenses of $45,000.

Required:

a. How many equivalent units of product were processed this year?

b. What was the cost per equivalent gallon of tea processed this year?

c. Bottling incurred how much total cost this period?

d. How many equivalent units of product did bottling produce this period?

e. What is the cost per equivalent unit for bottling this period?

f. Based on the definition of product cost used by traditional cost measurement systems (direct materials, direct labor, manufacturing overhead) what is the cost per equivalent unit of tea completed this period?

g. Based on the broader definition of product cost used by contemporary cost measurement systems, what is the full cost of a gallon of tea this period considering production, administrative, and marketing costs?

h. What are the behavioral implications of the two different product cost calculations you have done in parts (f) and (g) of this problem?

11. The American Association of University Women (AAUW) provides college scholarships for economically disadvantaged high school graduates. The AAUW grants scholarships based on applications filed by students. The following table shows the activities involved in evaluating an application and the approximate percentage of total processing effort consumed by each activity.

Activity	Percent of Total Processing
Receive and log application	10%
Enter into computer evaluation template	10
Send letters of verification	20
Update file and print evaluation score	10
Rank applicants and grant scholarships	40
Notify and disburse funds	10

In the first year of the program, the scholarship committee received 800 applications. Of these the committee completely processed 650 during the first year. The remaining applications had been received and logged, but no additional processing steps had been performed at the end of year 1. In the second year the committee received 900 additional applications. At the end of year 2, one hundred applications were partially processed. One-half of these had been received and logged; the other half had letters of verification sent.

Required:

a. On an equivalent units basis, how many scholarship applications did the committee process during year 1?

b. On an equivalent units basis, how many scholarship applications did the committee process during year 2?

c. From the perspective of the scholarship applicant, what constitutes quality in the process of granting scholarships?

d. What quality measures might you suggest that the committee track?

e. What is the time required for the scholarship application process? (Think in terms of the customer's perspective of time.)

12. Refer to the previous problem. Assume you work for University of the South. One of your jobs is to prepare advertising materials and supervise application processing for AAUW. You are also responsible for managing the costs of its operations. The work you do for AAUW uses about 20 percent of your time, and AAUW reimburses your university for 20 percent of your salary. AAUW receives free space for this operation from University of the South, and faculty members donated old computers, file cabinets, desks, and other office equipment. Your major cost item is payroll. You don't have any permanent employees, but students serve as temporary employees when processing has to be performed. In addition, you have supplies, telephone, and advertising expenses. The costs incurred in years 1 and 2 are as follows:

Expenditure Item	Year 1	Year 2	Comments
Salaries	$7,000	$10,275	Part time wages of college students.
Telephone	600	750	Monthly charge of $50 levied by the university plus extra service features installed.
Supplies	875	1,283	Used on each application.
Advertising	1,500	2,000	The AAUW committee approved a higher budget in year 2.
Manager's salary	7,000	7,210	Twenty percent of manager's salary and benefits.

Required:

a. What was the cost per application processed in year 1?

b. What was the cost per application processed in year 2?

c. How well is the manager managing the cost of the operation? (Hint: Think about how costs would behave as the volume of applications change.)

d. The industry norm for processing applications is about $15 per application. Given the cost structure that exists for this operation, how many applications must AAUW process to achieve the industry norm?

Writing Assignments

13. You have been hired as project manager for financial systems at an old-line *Fortune* 500 manufacturing firm and want to get approval for an activity/operation costing project. However, your boss, who has been with the firm for 37 years, argues that the firm has been profitable for 50 years without this "new-fangled accounting" and there is no need for a new system. Write a memo to persuade the boss. Remember, she does your performance evaluation, so you must be very tactful.

14. Explain two ways in which financial reporting principles have influenced the focus of traditional cost measurement systems.

Team Projects

15. Visit a local business. Determine what its key strategic decisions are, define relevant cost objects for each, and design a set of account codes for its cost measurement system.

16. Identify a *Fortune* 500 firm that you would expect to use job order costing. Visit its website or obtain a copy of its annual report to see whether you can deduce what kinds of jobs it would need to account for. What cost items should it trace to jobs? Are there any costs the firm should not trace to jobs?

17. Visit a local firm and draw a process map of its production process similar to that shown in Exhibit 10 of the module. Describe activities and operations the firm must perform to produce its product or provide its service to customers and define a set of account codes to track costs to each.

▲ PROBLEMS AND CASES—ADVANCED LEVEL

18. The Boys Club of Boone County operates two programs designed to keep at-risk teenagers out of trouble—an after-school program and a summer camp. In addition, staff members conduct numerous fund-raising events during the year, such as open houses at the club and a family day of activities for children of donors. For financial reporting purposes, the Boys Club is classified as a voluntary health and welfare organization (VHWO) and is subject to the standards of the Governmental Accounting Standards Board (GASB). The GASB requires all VHWOs to prepare an annual Statement of Functional Expenses that shows spending separately by the broad categories of program spending and supporting services. Supporting services expenditures are further subdivided into management/general and fund-raising. The club's cost measurement system is designed to facilitate compliance with this reporting requirement as well as to provide information to help manage costs in these areas. Accordingly, the cost measurement system uses these four cost objects:

> Program spending, after-school program
> Program spending, summer camp
> Supporting services, management and general
> Supporting services, fund-raising

You have recently been hired as a part-time student intern to help with the club's accounting. From the club's records you have obtained the following information about resources consumed during the past year of operation.

Cost Elements	Amount
Direct labor	
Sports director	8,800
Art teacher	7,200
Camp counselors	9,000
Bus driver	14,000
Custodian	22,000
Other operating expenses	
Manager's salary	44,000
Travel	7,600
Van operating expenses	9,500
Printing and publicity	18,000
Rent	16,000
Utilities	3,500
Insurance	7,400
Phone	3,800
Supplies	4,200

The club's existing cost measurement system traces labor costs to cost objects on the basis of information provided by time sheets indicating the time spent on each program. For last year, the employee salaries traced to each program are as shown below.

Employee	After School	Camp	Management/ General	Fund- raising
Sports director	5,250	1,600	700	1,250
Art teacher	4,520	1,464	678	538
Camp counselors	0	9,000	0	0
Bus driver	8,400	4,900	0	700
Custodian	15,400	3,300	0	3,300

The club's existing cost measurement system assigns operating expenses (including the manager's salary) to the programs on the basis of direct labor costs. However, you have convinced the club manager to let you experiment with activity analysis and design a contemporary cost measurement system for the club. After much coaxing, you induce the manager to review his calendar and estimate how he spends his time. He determines that during the 42 weeks of the year when the after-school program is operating, he spends, on average, 15 hours per week in supervisory activities related to that program, 4 hours on developing programs for the summer camp, 11 hours on general management tasks, and 10 hours meeting with donors and other activities related to fund-raising. During the eight weeks when the summer camp is operating, he spends, on average, 6 hours per week in various activities related to the after-school program, 20 hours on the summer camp, 10 hours on general management tasks, and 4 hours in activities related to fund-raising. The remaining two weeks of the year the club is closed.

You determine that travel expenses, van operating expenses, and printing and publicity costs can be traced directly to cost objects. Analysis of travel reimbursement records reveals that the travel costs are distributed as follows: after-school program, $750; camp, $800; management and general, $3,500; and fund-raising, $2,550. In discussions with the driver, you estimate that the van drove 15,000 miles for the after-school program; 9,000 miles for the camp; 600 miles on miscellaneous errands for management; and 400 miles for fund-raising events. Invoices show charges for printing and publicity of $4,500 for the after-school program; $3,600 for the camp; $2,700 for management; and $7,200 for fund-raising.

All other indirect costs will be combined into a single cost pool and assigned on the basis of square feet occupied. You and the manager estimate that roughly 50 percent of the space is used by the after-school program, 20 percent for camp-related activities and storage, and 25 percent by general and administrative activities. The rest is used for records storage related to fund-raising .

A local corporation has offered to provide a major grant to help the club cover operating expenses. The company's bylaws stipulate that it may donate only to nonprofit organizations whose expenditures for items other than program services are less than 20 percent of their total budget.

Required:

a. Based on the club's existing cost measurement system, determine the cost of the after-school program, the summer camp, management/general expenditures, and fund-raising. Calculate the total cost for the two categories of program spending and supporting services. Calculate the percentage of the club's total expenditures in each category.

b. Determine the total cost of the after-school program, the summer camp, management/ general expenditures, and fund-raising as defined by the contemporary cost measurement system suggested earlier. Calculate the total cost for the two categories of program spending and supporting services. Calculate the percentage of the club's total expenditures in each category.

c. Which system better helps management understand the resources consumed by the various programs?

d. The club's bookkeeper has suggested that rather than combine facilities costs (rent, utilities, insurance) with supplies and phone in a single cost pool, the system should use two cost pools, with the facilities cost allocated on the basis of square feet and the phone and supplies allocated on the basis of salaries. What is your response to this suggestion?

e. The manager rejects the new system because the new cost assignment means that the club will not qualify for the gift. The manager justifies this action by saying. "Allocations are all arbitrary, and there's no way to prove that one is any better than another." Write a memo to the club director, who has no accounting background, explaining your position on which system the club should use.

f. Comment on the behavioral and cultural issues raised by this situation.

19. A.P. Brown Industries (APB) is a small firm that produces five-speed transmissions for sale to specialty automakers such as Porsche and Lamborghini. The accountant is preparing a cost of production report for 1997. During 1997 the firm incurred $301,000 in materials costs and $129,000 in conversion costs. At the beginning of the year, it was working on 65 transmissions that were approximately 20 percent completed at that time. During the year work began on 180 transmissions. At the end of the year, the firm had 80 partly completed transmissions on the shop floor. The production supervisor believes these units are 30 percent complete.

Last year's cost per equivalent unit for transmissions was $2,400. The production manager receives a year-end bonus based on cost control. If this year's cost per equivalent unit is higher than last year's, he will receive no bonus. He is pressuring the supervisor to report a higher percentage of completion for the ending inventory in order to reduce the calculated cost per equivalent unit.

Required:

a. What is this year's cost per equivalent unit?

b. What must the percentage of completion of the year-end work-in-process be for the manager to qualify for a bonus?

c. How could the manager's performance be evaluated to avoid this adverse behavioral impact?

20. Reider Processing, Inc. manufactures food products, primarily vegetable oils. Its main customers are restaurant chains and grocery stores. Various crude oils (corn, soybean, palm) are purchased on long-term contracts. Because of the fluctuating prices in commodities markets, speculative buying of raw materials is key to maintaining profitability. Trading specialists monitor commodities markets continually, locking in long-term contracts when prices are favorable. Contracts specify price and delivery date, but Reider does not actually take delivery until the oils are needed.

All oils go through four processing steps: refining, bleaching, deodorizing, and hydrogenization. Oils for industrial customers such as Frito Lay are piped directly into tank trucks for delivery. Oils for restaurant chains such as Arby's and McDonald's are packaged in 35-gallon barrels.

Reider uses a traditional process costing system for its main production. At the beginning of the year, 125,000,000 gallons of vegetable oil were in process. These were approximately 40 percent processed. Costs incurred in the prior period on the oil in beginning work-in-process include $24,375,000 in materials and $5,900,000 in conversion costs. During the year, 400,000,000 gallons of oil were placed into production. At the end of the year, the firm had 90,000,000 gallons in work-in-process. These were about 55 percent processed. Accounting records show that Reider spent $88,000,000 for materials and $55,890,000 for conversion costs during the year.

Required:

a. Assume that all materials are added at the beginning of the process. Determine the cost per equivalent unit (gallon) for materials using the FIFO cost flow assumption. (Round your answers to four decimal places.)

b. Assume that conversion costs are incurred evenly throughout the process. Determine the cost per equivalent unit (gallon) for conversion costs using the FIFO cost flow assumption. (Round your answers to four decimal places.)

21. Although Reider (refer to previous question) is tiny, it has been able to compete successfully with such giant food processors as Cargill and Archer Daniels Midland by providing quick turnaround on special orders. For pricing special orders Reider uses a job-order costing system with costs assigned to jobs on the basis of activities performed to complete the job. Records provide the following information about activity costs, cost drivers, and units of the cost drivers.

Activities	Cost	Cost Driver	Units of Cost Driver
Commodities trades	$988,000	Time, hours	3,800
Receiving	1,128,000	Incoming shipments	1,200
Materials management	23,760,000	Materials cost	88,000,000
Refining	12,960,000	Batch	180
Bleaching	11,700,000	Batch	180
Deodorizing	19,800,000	Batch	180
Hydrogenization	6,300,000	Batch	180
Lab tests	3,510,000	No. of tests	3,600
Finished goods storage	15,229,000	No. of barrels	2,600,000
Delivery	10,625,000	Truckloads	3,400

During a recent flood in the Midwest, Cargill asked Reider for 15,000,000 gallons of oil because Cargill's plants were flooded and it was unable to meet commitments to its customers. Michelle Reider, the president of the firm, estimates that traders will need about four hours to locate and purchase the necessary oils on the spot market. The crude oil can be shipped to Reider in three shipments. Production personnel indicate the order will be processed in five batches. Because of Cargill's strict quality requirements eight lab tests will be needed to ensure adequate quality control. Because the oil will be piped directly from the production vats to the delivery truck, no finished goods storage is needed. The order will be delivered to Cargill in two truckloads. The cost of ingredients for the order is estimated to be $3,300,000.

Required:

a. Determine the total cost of all activities necessary to fill the Cargill order.

b. Use the activity cost analysis and estimated materials cost to determine the total cost per gallon of the oil produced for Cargill.

c. Why is the cost per gallon for the Cargill order different from the cost per gallon you calculated in (b)?

d. What factors other than cost should Reider use in deciding whether to accept the Cargill order?

e. Based on your answers to these two problems, should Reider accept the Cargill order? Why or why not?

Case 1: Yamazoo Waverunner Manufacturers.

Yamazoo manufactures two models of waverunners in its Kalamazoo, Michigan, plant: the Stingray and the Shark. The Shark has a larger engine and is generally more costly than the Stingray. Yamazoo's income statement for the year 1997 is shown in Exhibit 1. In 1997 it sold 2,000 Stingrays and 975 Sharks to waverunner dealers. These units were sold to dealers at approximately 200 percent of Yamazoo's manufacturing or product cost.

Dealers sell the waverunners to customers and perform warranty repairs for Yamazoo, during the one-year warranty period, using parts obtained from Yamazoo. Yamazoo pays dealers for labor and overhead at standard rates established for each type of repair performed. During the warranty period, an average of $75 is paid to dealers for warranty repairs for Stingrays and an average of $90 is paid for Sharks.

Internally, Yamazoo is divided into three production areas: engine assembly, final assembly, and special finishing. Each engine assembly cell is staffed by three highly trained, flexible employees who fully assemble and inspect engines. Shark engines spend approximately twice the time in engine assembly as Stingrays. Final assembly is a production line operation with lesser skilled employees who routinely perform the same assembly step on each waverunner. Both waverunner models receive the same processing and parts in this area. Stingrays are complete after final assembly; they do not receive special finishing. Sharks go through both assembly areas and also through special finishing. Stingrays and Sharks have different direct materials as well. The costing system captured the following information about production during 1997:

Description	Job Order 101	Job Order 102
Number and model of waverunner	1,000 sharks	2,000 Stingrays
Direct materials:		
Engine parts	$300,000	$220,000
Waverunner parts other than engines	200,000	300,000

In addition, engine assembly, final assembly, and special finishing incurred $300,000; $450,000; and $50,000; respectively, in other costs. During this period, special finishing was the only area with work-in-process inventory. It started the period with no inventory, and it completed only 975 units. The other remaining waverunners were 50 percent complete with respect to special finishing.

In addition to the manufacturing process, Yamazoo has an internal administrative office that performs normal personnel, accounting, and other administrative functions. Auditing, tax planning and preparation, and legal services are handled by outside contractors. The president of Yamazoo also contracts all product design and marketing services to outside agencies.

During this past year an external product design firm worked extensively with the Shark. It had engine problems that were corrected in the 1997 model. The design firm estimated that 80 percent of its effort was devoted to Sharks and that the remaining 20 percent went to developing the 1997 Stingray.

About 50 percent of all marketing costs were for the benefit of both products last year. Of the remaining 50 percent, the marketing firm spent 300 hours developing new manuals for the redesigned 1997 Shark and 150 hours reviewing and refreshing literature for the 1997 Stingray model.

Exhibit 21
Yamazoo Manufacturers

Income Statement For the fiscal year ended 12/31/97			
Sales Revenue			$3,599,450
Cost of Goods Sold			
Materials	$1,007,500		
Indirect Labor	259,864		
Factory Depreciation	232,500		
Rent & Utilities	150,000		
Tools & Supplies	99,500		
Insurance	50,000		1,799,364
Gross Profit			1,800,086
Warranty Expenses		$237,750	
Marketing		150,000	
Design Charges		100,000	
Outside Accounting		50,000	
Legal Services		25,000	
Common Carrier (delivery charges)		150,000	
Administrative Office Costs:			
Office Rent	48,000		
Salaries	250,000		
Depreciation, Office Equipment	16,000		
Utilities	16,000		
Insurance	30,000		
Supplies	50,000		
Telephone	40,000	450,000	$1,162,750
			637,336
Taxes			254,934
Profit after tax			$382,402

Required:

a. What is the conversion cost in engine assembly for a Shark engine? What is the cost for a Stingray engine?

b. What is the conversion cost per unit in final assembly if both Sharks and Stingrays require the same time, effort, and cost factors?

c. How many equivalent units of Sharks are complete with respect to special finishing?

d. What is the cost per unit in special finishing?

e. What is the product cost of a Shark and a Stingray?

f. How much marketing cost would you allocate to each product line? Why?

g. How would you suggest that common carrier cost should be allocated to each product? Why?

h. Using units of production to allocate all indirect costs that do not have a clear allocation base suggested in the problem, determine the full cost of a Shark and a Stingray. Considering this cost, what is the return on sales from selling one of each?

Case 2: Logic Conductors.[©]

> The semiconductor business is extremely competitive and rapidly changing. We need to choose our products and processes carefully. We are under extreme cost pressures and always welcome opportunities to reduce or manage our costs better. If we are not cost competitive, we will not last very long in this business. We need a good operations cost system not only to tell us what our products cost, but also to help us understand how each step in our production process contributes to that cost.

This is how the chief manufacturing engineer of Logic Conductors, Bangkok, Thailand, described the nature of the firm's business. Logic Conductors is an international manufacturer of electronic components such as circuit boards, semiconductors, cables, and connectors. It has manufacturing facilities throughout the United States, Asia, and Europe. Its Asian manufacturing operations are in Thailand, Malaysia, Hong Kong, and Singapore. Corporate offices are located in the United States. Regional headquarters make the sales and then assign production to plants based on their location and manufacturing capability. The company's current sales exceed $5,000,000,000 and it employs more than 30,000 people. Half of its sales are from North America. The other half is split evenly between Europe and Asia.

Products.

Semiconductors, or chips in common parlance, are integrated circuits usually made out of silicon. High-precision chips, though, use other materials such as gallium arsenide. Semiconductor chips vary in sophistication from simple "merchant" semiconductors to sophisticated application-specific integrated circuits (ASICs). Merchant semiconductors are integrated circuits used in simple electronic applications such as telephones, kitchen appliances, and sophisticated children's toys. They are typically mass produced in large batches. Next in terms of complexity and sophistication are dynamic random access memory (DRAM) chips used in personal computers and peripherals. ASICs are dedicated to specific applications and, therefore, are produced in smaller lot sizes. Logic produces mostly sophisticated DRAM memory chips and ASICs in its wafer-fabrication facility in Bangkok.

Fabrication Process.

The fabrication process for the various types of chips reflects their level of sophistication. Typically, the fabrication process is defined by the distance between the number of transistors packed on a chip. For example, Intel's Pentium II chip introduced in 1997 has several million more transistors than the Pentium introduced in 1995. The distance between each transistor on the Pentium was .35 microns. The Pentium II has been fabricated on a new process that packs the chips at .25 microns or much closer together.

Given the nature of its product line, the company produces a large variety of integrated circuits in small lot sizes. Its design facility in California does the basic design and lithography of the chips. In the lithography process a blank wafer coated with light-sensitive material is exposed to the circuit pattern. A laser-etching machine transfers the circuit design onto a "wafer," which is then doped with solvents and stripped away until the circuit design is etched on the wafer. The etched wafer, which contains several dies, is the basic raw material for the Bangkok plant whose process starts with the receipt and storage of wafers. Exhibit 22 shows a simplified schematic diagram of the most important manufacturing operations.

The first step in the manufacturing process is to cut each die on the wafers with a diamond saw. A resin bonds the good dies to a backing in the cavity of the ceramic package. The dies are then mounted on a frame and a threading machine attaches metal wires (aluminum, silver, or gold) that act as the inserts that connect the chip to the external electrical connection in the end product. The cutting operation, which is next, cuts the wires to the exact size called out in the product specification. The stamping operation puts an ink stamp on each chip that identifies the type of chip and its manufacturing location. The last step is a test to ensure that all connections are functioning; this step also burns in the chips in electronic ovens to ensure stability in the operating environment for that application. The special ovens typically take batches of 200 chips at any one time.

Exhibit 22
Manufacturing Layout for Bangkok Plant

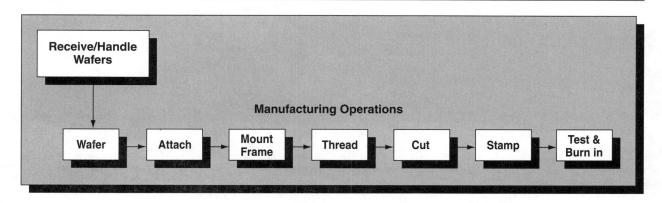

Each manufacturing operation has one machine operator. One supervisor and one manufacturing engineer oversee the entire manufacturing operation.

At each stage of the manufacturing process, the yields are different. Of the wafers introduced in the production process, only 90 to 92 percent reach the resin-attachment operation. Another 5 to 6 percent of the chips are lost between resin attachment and stamping. Finally, the test stage usually uncovers another 1 percent defective so that the final yield is typically much lower than the number of wafers put into process during any given period.

Cost Data.

In the early 1990s, responding to increased competition on both price and quality in the electronics industry, Logic Conductors instituted a TQM program. The program was well received and cascaded training was used to get the message to every level in the organization. Within two years a quality focus had emerged, but costs were still not under control.

The company's cost system was typical of most traditional job-order costing systems. It identified materials cost based on requisitions. Labor time tickets were used to assign labor costs. For manufacturing overhead costs the system traced them first to departments and then assigned them to customer jobs using predetermined rates. While all manufacturing operations were in one department, the manufacturing overhead was divided into two cost pools. The first pool included materials handling and supervision. These costs were allocated to jobs based on direct labor hours. The other pool included the remaining costs, and machine hours were the base for allocating these costs. There was a growing feeling that the system was not providing the type of cost data needed for cost management.

To solve this problem the company began to implement an activity-based cost system to determine cost of the products and cost of each manufacturing operation (activity). The new system traced all resources to activities and manufacturing operations. Next the system identified a resource and cost driver for each activity and operation. The cost drivers were used to assign costs to products. The last step was to create cost pools based on common drivers.

This last year the total manufacturing cost was $540,500 broken down as follows:

Cost Item	Total
Machine operator salaries	$88,000
Supervisor salaries—material handling	12,000
Supervisor salaries—manufacturing	35,000
Machine depreciation	370,000
Occupancy	28,000
Supplies	4,800
Furniture/fixtures	2,700
Total cost	**$540,500**

The following additional information is also available.

1. Operator salaries and machine depreciation for each operation are as follows:

	Material Handling	Saw	Resin	Frame	Wire	Cut	Stamp	Test	Total
Salaries	$10,500	12,500	10,500	12,500	13,000	11,400	9,600	8,000	88,000
Machine depreciation		55,000	65,000	35,000	50,000	24,000	16,000	125,000	370,000

2. The manufacturing supervisors spend equal time on all operations.

3. Space occupied by the equipment in each operation is as follows:

	Material Handling	Saw	Resin	Frame	Wire	Cut	Stamp	Test	Total
Percentage of total space	14%	11	11	10	15	11	9	19	100

4. All activities and operations have roughly the same use of supplies.

5. Each employee is provided with furniture and fixtures. The cost is approximately 2 percent of their salary.

6. The following table provides cost drivers for each activity and operation. Also available are total amount of each driver consumed and the amount consumed by two of the many jobs done this last year. Job 1 produced video dynamic random access memory (VDRAM) chips for a manufacturer of PC video cards. Job 2 is a digital signal processor (DSP) chip for use in a cellular telephone/beeper combination device.

Activity/Manufacturing Operation	Cost Driver	Drivers Consumed by All Jobs	Drivers Consumed By	
			Job 1 VDRAM	Job 2 DSP
Material handling	# of units	300,000	20,000	28,000
Saw cut	# of saw cuts	1,750,000	2	3
Resin	# of wafers	250,000	18,000	26,000
Frame	# of framing hours	6,750	1 minute	2 minutes
Wire	# of inserts	5,000,000	12	8
Cut	# of wire cuts	750,000	4	2
Stamp	# of items stamped	230,000	17,000	25,000
Test	# of hours	7,245	75 min	120 min

7. The raw material cost of the wafer for the two jobs was

Chip job 1	$11.45 per wafer
Chip job 2	14.56 per wafer

8. Both jobs were complete at the end of the period.

Required:

a. Compute the total cost of each manufacturing operation at Logic Conductors. Do you think there might be better ways of tracing resources to operations?

b. Do you think it is appropriate for the new system to lump labor with the other manufacturing support costs and assign it to products as a single number?

c. Which management insight does this calculation provide? How might you use this information for cost management?

d. For each manufacturing operation, compute a cost per driver.

e. Which management insight does this calculation provide? How might you use this information for cost management?

f. Compute the unit product cost for the two jobs. What is the impact of "yield" rate on unit product cost?

LIST OF MODULES

MANAGEMENT ACCOUNTING—A STRATEGIC FOCUS, A MODULAR SERIES

Currently Available:

Strategy and Management Accounting (0-256-27147-X)
Management Accounting in the Age of Lean Production (0-256-27146-1)
Target Costing (0-256-27145-3)
Measuring and Managing Environmental Costs (0-256-27144-5)
Measuring and Managing Quality Costs (0-256-27143-7)
Activity-Based Management (0-256-23787-5)
Measuring and Managing Capacity (0-256-27141-0)
Measuring and Managing Indirect Costs (0-256-27140-2)
Manufacturing Overhead Allocation: Traditional and Activity Based (0-256-26392-2)
The Organizational Role of Management Accountants (0-256-26395-7)
Activity-Based Budgeting (0-256-26393-0)
The Theory of Constraints and Throughput Accounting (0-07027589-0)
Cost Measurement Systems: Traditional and Contempory Approaches (0-256-26394-9)

Forthcoming Modules:

The Kaleidoscopic Nature of Costs: Cost Terms and Classifications
International Managerial Accounting
Managing Supply Chain and Make or Buy Decisions
Benchmarking for Competitor and Value Chain Analysis
Activity Based Marketing and Distribution Cost Analysis
Cost Management Using Business Process Reengineering
Cost Analysis for Pricing and Capacity Use Decisions
Cost Profit Product Mix and Volume Analysis
Product Costing in Mass Manufacturing-Process Costing
Job Costing in Mass and Lean Manufacturing Environments
Product Costing in Lean Manufacturing-Operations Costing
Joint Cost Problems in Manufacturing and Service Industries
Strategic Budgeting Part II: Multi-year Product and Profit Planning
Strategic Budgeting Part III: Long-term Capital Budgeting
Customer Profitability Analysis
Driver Based Cost Estimation Methods
Experience Based Cost Estimation Methods
Standard and Kaizen Costing
Variance Analysis
Analyzing Throughout, Mix and Yield
Inventory Management in Mass and Lean Environments
Capacity Rationing Using Linear Programming
The Historical Evolution of Cost Accounting
Absorption Cost vs. Variable Cost Systems
Management Accounting Systems and Information Technology
Measuring Preproduction Costs

PRICING AND PACKAGING

Effective immediately, all modules are priced at $4.95 list ($3.95 net). The STRATEGY AND MANAGEMENT ACCOUNTING module can be downloaded for free from our modules homepage:
http//www.mhhe.com/business/accounting/modules.
Hard copies are available on request.